CONGRESSIONAL POLICIES, PRACTICES AND PROCEDURES

U.S. HOUSE OF REPRESENTATIVES

ETHICS ENFORCEMENT AND DISCIPLINE

CONGRESSIONAL POLICIES, PRACTICES AND PROCEDURES

Additional books in this series can be found on Nova's website under the Series tab.

Additional E-books in this series can be found on Nova's website under the E-book tab.

ETHICAL ISSUES IN THE 21ST CENTURY

Additional books in this series can be found on Nova's website under the Series tab.

Additional E-books in this series can be found on Nova's website under the E-book tab.

CONGRESSIONAL POLICIES, PRACTICES AND PROCEDURES

U.S. HOUSE OF REPRESENTATIVES

ETHICS ENFORCEMENT AND DISCIPLINE

BRUNO MONTAGNE
EDITOR

nova publishers
New York

For permission to use material from this book please contact us:
Telephone 631-231-7269; Fax 631-231-8175
Web Site: http://www.novapublishers.com

Library of Congress Cataloging-in-Publication Data

ISBN: 978-1-62808-364-4

Published by Nova Science Publishers, Inc. † New York

CONTENTS

PREFACE

The United States Constitution provides each House of Congress with the sole authority to establish rules, judge membership requirements, and punish and expel Members. From 1789 to 1967, the House of Representatives dealt with disciplinary action against Members on a case-by-case basis, often forming ad-hoc committees to investigate and make recommendations when acts of wrongdoing were brought to the chamber's attention. Events of the 1960's, including the investigation of Representative Adam Clayton Powell for alleged misuse of Education and Labor Committee funds, prompted the creation of a permanent ethics committee and the writing of the Code of Conduct for Members, officers, and staff of the House. This book outlines the background of ethics enforcement in the House of Representatives, including the creation of both the Select Committee on Ethics and the Committee on Ethics. The book also focuses on various jurisdictional and procedural changes that the committee has experienced since 1967 and discusses the committee's current jurisdiction and procedures.

Chapter 1 – The United States Constitution (Article 1, Section 5, clause 1) provides each House of Congress with the sole authority to establish rules, judge membership requirements, and punish and expel Members. From 1789 to 1967, the House of Representatives dealt with disciplinary action against Members on a case-by-case basis, often forming ad-hoc committees to investigate and make recommendations when acts of wrongdoing were brought to the chamber’s attention. Events of the 1960’s, including the investigation of Representative Adam Clayton Powell for alleged misuse of Education and Labor Committee funds, prompted the creation of a permanent ethics committee and the writing of a Code of Conduct for Members, officers, and staff of the House.

Begun as a select committee in the 89th Congress (1965-1966), the House created a 12-member panel to "recommend to the House ... such ... rules or regulations ... necessary or desirable to insure proper standards of conduct by Members of the House and by officers and employees of the House, in the performance of their duties and the discharge of their responsibilities." Acting on the select committee's recommendations, the House created a permanent Committee on Standards of Official Conduct in the 90th Congress (1967-1968). In the 112th Congress (2011- 2012), the committee was renamed the Committee on Ethics.

This report briefly outlines the background of ethics enforcement in the House of Representatives, including the creation of both the Select Committee on Ethics and the Committee on Ethics. The report also focuses on various jurisdictional and procedural changes that the committee has experienced since 1967 and discusses the committee's current jurisdiction and procedures.

Chapter 2 – The House Office of Congressional Ethics (OCE) was established on March 11, 2008, with the passage of H.Res. 895. It was reauthorized by the House as part of the rules package (H.Res. 5) adopted by the 113th Congress on January 3, 2013.

This action followed years of efforts by groups within and outside Congress to create an independent entity to investigate allegations of misconduct by members, officers, and employees of Congress. During the 110th Congress (2007-2008), Speaker of the House Nancy Pelosi and Minority Leader John Boehner created the bipartisan Special Task Force on Ethics Enforcement, chaired by Representative Michael Capuano, to consider whether the House should create an "outside" ethics-enforcement entity. The task force worked for nearly a year before issuing its recommendations for the creation of the OCE.

The mandate of the OCE, which has jurisdiction only in the House, is to review information, and when appropriate, refer findings of fact to the House Committee on Ethics. Only this committee, pursuant to House rules, has the authority to recommend House discipline of members and staff. Information of alleged wrongdoing by members, officers, and employees of the House may be accepted by the OCE from the general public, but only the OCE board can initiate a review.

The OCE is composed of six board members, and at least two alternates, each of whom serves a four-year term. The Speaker and the minority leader are each responsible for the appointment of three board members and one alternate. The chair is selected by the Speaker and a co-chair is selected by the minority leader. Current members of the House, federal employees, and lobbyists are not eligible to serve on the board.

OCE rules for the conduct of investigations and code of conduct can be found at their website, http://oce.house.gov.

This report describes the history and rationale behind the creation of the OCE, its operations, and its relationship with the House Committee on Ethics, and options potentially available for Congress if further amendments to the House ethics process are desired.

Chapter 3 – The House of Representatives—in the same manner as the United States Senate—is expressly authorized within the United States Constitution (Article I, Section 5, clause 2) to discipline or "punish" its own Members. This authority of the House to discipline a Member for "disorderly Behaviour" is in addition to any criminal or civil liability that a Member of the House may incur for particular misconduct, and is used not merely to punish an individual Member, but to protect the institutional integrity of the House of Representatives, its proceedings, and its reputation.

The House may discipline its Members without the necessity of Senate concurrence. The most common forms of discipline in the House are now "expulsion," "censure," or "reprimand"; although the House may also discipline its Members in other ways, including fine or monetary restitution, loss of seniority, and suspension or loss of certain privileges. In addition to such sanctions imposed by the full House of Representatives, the standing committee in the House which deals with ethics and official conduct matters, the House Committee on Ethics—formerly called the Committee on Standards of Official Conduct—is authorized by House Rules to issue a formal "Letter of Reproval" for misconduct which does not rise to the level of consideration or sanction by the entire House of Representatives. Additionally, the Committee on Ethics has also expressed its disapproval of certain conduct in informal letters and communications to Members.

The House may generally discipline its Members for violations of statutory law, including crimes; for violations of internal congressional rules; or for any conduct which the House of Representatives finds has reflected discredit upon the institution. Thus, each house of Congress has disciplined its own Members for conduct which has not necessarily violated any specific rule or law, but which was found to breach its privileges, demonstrate contempt for the institution, or reflect discredit on the House or Senate. When the most severe sanction of expulsion has been employed in the House of Representatives, however, the underlying conduct deemed by the House to have merited removal from office has historically involved either disloyalty to the United States Government, or the violation of a criminal law involving the abuse of one's official position, such as bribery. The House of Representatives has actually expelled only five Members in its history, but a number of Members, facing likely congressional discipline for various forms of misconduct, have resigned from Congress prior to any formal House action or leave office after election defeat.

Chapter 4 – House Rule XI, clause 1(d), requires each committee to submit to the House, not later than July 1 and December 31 of each year, a report on the activities of that committee under that rule and House Rule X during the Congress ending on January 3 of that year. This report summarizes the activities of the Committee on Ethics for the semiannual period ending December 31, 2012, as well as for the entirety of the 112th Congress.

The jurisdiction of the Committee on Ethics ("Committee") is defined in clauses 1(g) and 11(g)(4) of House Rule X, clause 3 of House Rule XI, and clause 5(h) of House Rule XXV.

In: U.S. House of Representatives
Editor: Bruno Montagne

ISBN: 978-1-62808-364-4

Chapter 1

HOUSE COMMITTEE ON ETHICS: A BRIEF HISTORY OF ITS EVOLUTION AND JURISDICTION*

Jacob R. Straus

SUMMARY

The United States Constitution (Article 1, Section 5, clause 1) provides each House of Congress with the sole authority to establish rules, judge membership requirements, and punish and expel Members. From 1789 to 1967, the House of Representatives dealt with disciplinary action against Members on a case-by-case basis, often forming ad-hoc committees to investigate and make recommendations when acts of wrongdoing were brought to the chamber's attention. Events of the 1960's, including the investigation of Representative Adam Clayton Powell for alleged misuse of Education and Labor Committee funds, prompted the creation of a permanent ethics committee and the writing of a Code of Conduct for Members, officers, and staff of the House.

Begun as a select committee in the 89th Congress (1965-1966), the House created a 12-member panel to "recommend to the House ... such ... rules or regulations ... necessary or desirable to insure proper standards of conduct by Members of the House and by officers and employees of the

* This is an edited, reformatted and augmented version of a Congressional Research Service publication, CRS Report for Congress 98-15, prepared for Members and Committees of Congress, from www.crs.gov, dated March 7, 2013.

House, in the performance of their duties and the discharge of their responsibilities." Acting on the select committee's recommendations, the House created a permanent Committee on Standards of Official Conduct in the 90th Congress (1967-1968). In the 112th Congress (2011- 2012), the committee was renamed the Committee on Ethics.

This report briefly outlines the background of ethics enforcement in the House of Representatives, including the creation of both the Select Committee on Ethics and the Committee on Ethics. The report also focuses on various jurisdictional and procedural changes that the committee has experienced since 1967 and discusses the committee's current jurisdiction and procedures.

INTRODUCTION

In the *Federalist Papers*, James Madison noted the importance of participation by upstanding citizens at all levels of government as a condition for legitimate governance. "The aim of every political constitution is, or ought to be, first to obtain for rulers men who possess most wisdom to discern, and most virtue to pursue, the common good of the society; and in the next place, to take the most effectual precautions for keeping them virtuous whilst they continue to hold their public trust."[1]

To ensure that Members uphold high standards, the Constitution provides each House of Congress sole authority to establish rules, judge membership requirements, and punish and expel its Members. Article I, Section 5, clause 1 provides that "Each House shall be the Judge of the Elections, Returns, and Qualifications of its own Members."[2] In addition, clause 2 provides that "Each House may determine the Rules of its Proceedings, punish its Members for disorderly Behaviour, and, with the Concurrence of two thirds, expel a Member."[3] Congress used their ability to establish ethics rules and to punish individual Members sparingly in the 18th and 19th centuries.[4]

As former Senate historian Richard Baker observed on the subject of congressional ethics, "[f]or nearly two centuries, a simple and informal code of behavior existed. Prevailing norms of general decency served as the chief determinants of proper legislative conduct."[5] During that time, Congress often dealt with potential ethics issues "on a case-by-case basis, only with the most obvious acts of wrongdoing, those clearly 'inconsistent with the trust and duty of a member.'"[6] Events in the 1960s, including the investigation of Representative Adam Clayton Powell's alleged misuse of Education and Labor Committee funds,[7] prompted a special subcommittee of the Committee on House Administration to investigate the allegations and the potential creation of an ethics committee to establish a code of conduct for the House of Representatives.[8]

This report examines the history and evolution of the House Committee on Ethics, including the committee's jurisdiction and investigative procedure. It does not deal with changes to federal or state criminal law or with criminal prosecutions of Members of Congress or with the specifics of disciplinary cases in the House.[9]

CREATING A PERMANENT ETHICS COMMITTEE

Prior to the creation of the House Committee on Standards of Official Conduct in the 90th Congress (1967-1968), no uniform mechanism existed for self-discipline in the House of Representatives. Congress, however, had previously attempted to create an ethical framework for House Members and employees. In 1958, Congress established the first Code of Ethics for Government Service.[10] Initially proposed in 1951 by Representative Charles Bennett, the Code of Ethics was adopted as a result of a House investigation of presidential chief of staff Sherman Adams, who was alleged to have received gifts from an industrialist being investigated by the Federal Trade Commission.[11] The Code of Ethics for Government Service standards continue to be recognized as ethical guidance in the House and Senate. They are, however, not legally binding because the code was adopted by congressional resolution, not by law.[12]

In the period preceding the creation of the Committee on Standards of Official Conduct in 1967, investigations into alleged wrongdoing by Members and staff of the House were dealt with in an ad-hoc fashion.[13] There were, however, attempts to create a more uniform system to investigate and discipline Members and staff.[14] For example, during hearings before the Joint Committee on the Organization of Congress in 1965, considerable testimony was presented on the ethical conduct of Members, and the need for House and Senate codes of conduct, financial disclosure regulations, and a House Ethics Committee (the Senate had created one in 1964).[15] In its final report, the Joint Committee called for the creation of a Committee on Standards and Conduct in the House.[16]

Select Committee on Standards and Conduct

On September 2, 1966, following publicized allegations of misconduct by House Education and Labor Committee Chair Adam Clayton Powell, Representative Charles Bennett introduced H.Res. 1013 to create a Select Committee on Standards and Conduct, which was referred to the Committee on Rules.[17] On September 7, the Committee on Rules reported the resolution "with the recommendation that the resolution do pass."[18] On October 19, the House debated, amended, and agreed to H.Res. 1013, creating the select committee.[19] As adopted, the resolution created a 12-member panel, with six majority and six minority Members appointed by the Speaker of the House. The Select Committee was charged with two duties. They were to

1) recommend to the House, by report or resolution such additional rules or regulations as the Select Committee shall determine to be necessary or desirable to insure proper standards of conduct by Members of the House and by officers or employees of the House, in the performance of their duties and the discharge of their responsibilities; and
2) report violations, by a majority vote of the Select Committee, of any law to the proper Federal and State authorities.[20]

Pursuant to H.Res. 1013, the report on the Select Committee's activities at the end of the 89th Congress (1965-1966) included recommendations for House action on ethics-related matters. Because the select committee only existed between October and December 1966, the committee concluded that they could not "prudently recommend changes in existing provisions of law or recommend new ones at this time."[21] Instead, they recommended that (1) the committee be continued as a select committee in the 90th Congress; (2) legislation introduced in the 90th Congress on standards and conduct should be referred to the select committee; and (3) Members of the House should be asked for suggested changes in existing statutes. In addition, the report included draft language for the continuation of the select committee.[22]

Committee on Standards of Official Conduct (Now Committee on Ethics)

In the first session of the 90th Congress (1967-1966), more than 100 resolutions were introduced to create a Committee on Standards of Official

Conduct. One of these proposals, H.Res. 18, was introduced on January 10, 1967, by Representative Charles Bennett, chair of the Select Committee on Standards and Conduct in the 89th Congress.[23] H.Res. 18 was referred to the Committee on Rules, which held a series of hearings on this, and other similar resolutions, in February and March 1967.[24]

During the hearings, the Committee on Rules heard from numerous Members of the House and considered proposals to create both a select and a standing committee on standards and conduct. Representative Bennett, the sponsor of H.Res. 18, argued that a standards committee would be essential to aid the House in dealing with issues of perceived and actual impropriety by Members. He testified:

> The public image of Congress demands that the House establish a full, working, thoughtful committee working solely in the field of standards and conduct. Sixty percent of those answering a recent Gallup poll said they believe the misuse of Government funds by Congressmen is fairly common. Of course, we know that such abuses are, in fact, not common, but we have seen a number of such damaging polls showing the people's lack of faith in the integrity of Congress.
>
> There is a need for a vehicle in the House to achieve and maintain the highest possible standards by statute and enforcement thereof. This can only be done after through study by a committee whose primary interests are in the field of ethics.[25]

On April 6, 1967, following its hearings on H.Res. 18 and other similar resolutions, the House Rules Committee reported H.Res. 418,[26] "to establish a standing committee to be known as the Committee on Standards of Official Conduct."[27]

On April 13, the House debated and passed H.Res. 418 by a vote of 400 to zero.[28] The resolution created a bipartisan 12-member standing committee with the initial mission to make "recommendations for its jurisdiction"[29] and to "recommend as soon as practicable to the House of Representatives such changes in laws, rules, and regulations as the committee deems necessary to establish and enforce standards of official conduct for Members, officers and employees of the House."[30] The first members of the committee were appointed on May 1 when H.Res. 457 (majority members)[31] and H.Res. 458 (minority members)[32] were agreed to by the House. The Committee on Standards of Official Conduct (Committee on Standards) held its first hearings in the summer and fall of 1967.[33] The hearings were designed to help the committee meet the requirements of H.Res. 418 "to write, and recommend to the House, a set of standards for the official conduct of the Chambers' Members and employees."[34]

In March 1968, the Committee issued a report summarizing their activities and recommending

- continuation of the committee as a select committee;
- changes in the committee's jurisdiction and powers;
- creation of a Code of Official Conduct and financial disclosure rules for Members, officers, and employees of the House;
- establishment of standardized controls by the Committee on House Administration over committees using counterpart funds (foreign currencies held by U.S. embassies that can only be spent in the country of origin);
- a prompt review of the Federal Corrupt Practices Act (reporting of campaign expenditures) by the House;[35] and
- compliance by House candidates with applicable provisions of the proposed Code of Official Conduct.[36]

On March 14, 1968, Representative Melvin Price, chair of the Committee on Standards, introduced H.Res. 1099 "to continue the Committee on Standards of Official Conduct as a permanent standing committee of the House of Representatives."[37]

The resolution was referred to the Committee on Rules, and was reported with amendments on April 1.[38]

On April 3, the Committee on Rules reported a special rule (H.Res. 1119) for the consideration of H.Res. 1099. Following adoption of H.Res. 1119, debate on H.Res. 1099 proceeded. In his opening statement, Representative Price discussed the reasons for amending H.Res. 418 and making the committee a permanent, standing committee of the House.

> The reason for amending that original resolution, as opposed to offering a completely new resolution, is that the committee felt it would be advantageous—from the standpoints of continuity and orderliness—to extend the life of the existing committee rather than constitute a new committee.[39]

Following the adoption of several amendments, H.Res. 1099 was agreed to by a vote of 406 to 1.[40] The resolution provided for (1) continuation of the

Committee on Standards as a permanent standing House committee; (2) enumeration of the committee's jurisdiction and powers; (3) creation of the first House Code of Official Conduct (Rule XLIII);[41] and (4) adoption of the first financial disclosure requirements for Members, officers, and designated employees (Rule XLIV).[42]

In the 112th Congress, the House renamed the Committee on Standards of Official Conduct to the Committee on Ethics.[43] The committee will be referred to as the Committee on Ethics for the remainder of this report.

JURISDICTION

In addition to establishing the Committee on Ethics as a permanent standing committee, H.Res. 1099 formalized the committee's jurisdiction. The *History of the United States House of Representatives, 1789-1994*, published by the Committee on House Administration in the 103rd Congress (1993-1994), summarized four major jurisdictional areas for the Committee on Ethics.

> Since 1968, the House has authorized and directed the Ethics Committee to: (1) recommend to the House legislative or administrative actions deemed necessary for establishing or enforcing standards of conduct; (2) investigate allegations of violations of the Code of Official Conduct or any law, rule, regulation, or other standard of conduct applicable to Members, officers, and employees in the performance of official duties; and after notice and a hearing, recommend to the House whatever action or sanctions it deems appropriate; (3) subject to House approval, report to appropriate state and federal authorities about evidence of violations of law by Members, officers, and employees in the performance of official duties;[44] and (4) issue and publish advisory opinions for the guidance of Members, officers, and employees.[45]

The committee was also provided with jurisdiction over the Code of Official Conduct and financial disclosure.[46]

In addition to establishing the committee's jurisdiction, H.Res. 1099, and subsequent amendments, imposed several constraints on the Committee on Ethics. These limits, except where noted, are still in effect in House Rule XI, clause 3(a). They stipulate that

- there must be an affirmative vote of seven out of 12 committee members for the issuance of any report, resolution, recommendation, or advisory opinion relating to the official conduct of a Member, officer, or employee or the investigation of such conduct;[47]
- investigations, other than those initiated by the committee, can be undertaken only upon receipt of a complaint, in writing and under oath, from a Member of the House, or an individual not a Member if the committee finds that such complaint has been submitted by the individual to no fewer than three Members who have refused in writing to transmit the complaint to the committee;[48]
- investigations of alleged violations of any law or rule that was not in effect at the time of the alleged violation are prohibited;[49] and
- members of the committee are not eligible to participate in any committee proceeding relating to their official conduct.[50]

H.Res. 1099 also empowered the committee to hold hearings, receive testimony, and issue subpoenas in the course of conducting an investigation.[51]

When discussing the jurisdiction of House committees, it is important to note that the House Parliamentarian is the sole definitive authority on questions relating to the jurisdiction of the chamber's committees and should be consulted for a formal opinion on any specific procedural question.[52]

Changes in Jurisdiction

Since the establishment of the Committee on Ethics as a permanent standing committee, the committee's jurisdiction has been amended a number of times. Each of these changes "necessitated following experience under prior rules"[53] and reflected the changing nature of ethics enforcement in the House.

Lobbying and Campaign Finance

On May 19, 1970, Representative William Colmer introduced H.Res. 1031 to amend then clause 19 of Rule XI of the House "with respect of lobbying practices and political campaign contributions affecting the House of Representatives."[54] The Committee on Rules reported the resolution on June 11,[55] and it was brought up for debate on July 8. Following debate, the resolution was adopted to give the Committee on Ethics formal jurisdiction over lobbying activities as well as those involving the raising, reporting, and use of campaign funds.[56]

Authority over campaign contributions, lobbying, and financial disclosure have subsequently been removed from the committee's jurisdiction. In the 94th Congress (1975-1976), the House transferred jurisdiction over campaign contributions to the Committee on House Administration as part of the rules package.[57] In the 95th Congress (1977-1978), the House transferred jurisdiction over lobbying to the Committee on the Judiciary[58] and jurisdiction over measures relating to financial disclosure was reassigned to the Committee on Rules.[59]

Rules of Conduct

On March 2, 1977, the House adopted H.Res. 287, which contained several amendments and additions to the House rules of conduct.[60] Included were the first requirement that financial disclosure be made public; limits on outside earned income and unofficial office accounts; and further restrictions on the acceptance of gifts, the use of the franking privilege, and limits on foreign travel.

Pursuant to H.Res. 287, the Committee on Ethics assumed jurisdiction over these additional areas and was authorized to maintain the public financial disclosure reports filed by Members, officers, and designated employees.[61] In addition, the House established a Select Committee on Ethics, chaired by Representative L. Richardson Preyer, to assist the Committee on Ethics with the implementation of the new rules.[62]

Additional Authorities

On July 14, 1977, the House agreed to H.Res. 658 and established the Permanent Select Committee on Intelligence.[63] The resolution also authorized the Committee on Ethics to "investigate an unauthorized disclosure of intelligence or intelligence-related information by a Member, officer, or employee of the House in violation of paragraph (c) and report to the House concerning any allegation which it finds to be substantiated."[64]

In August 1977, the Committee on Ethics was designated at the "employing agency" for the House.[65] Pursuant to P.L. 95-105, the Foreign Relations Authorization Act for FY 1978, the Committee was authorized to issue regulations governing the acceptance by House Members, personnel, and employees of gifts, trips, and decorations from foreign governments.[66]

Financial Disclosure

In 1978, the Ethics in Government Act began requiring government-wide public financial disclosure requirements.[67] Subsequently, with the adoption of the House rules for the 96th Congress (1979-1980), the provisions of the House financial disclosure rule were replaced by those of the Ethics Act and incorporated into House rules.[68] This act delegated to the Committee on Ethics review, interpretation, and compliance responsibilities for the public financial disclosure reports that henceforth were to be filed with the Clerk of the House.

On April 4, 2012, the STOCK Act (Stop Trading on Congressional Knowledge Act) was passed to affirm that no exemption exists from "insider trading" laws and regulations for Members of Congress and congressional employees.[69] Pursuant to the act, the House Committee on Ethics (and the Senate Select Committee on Ethics) is required to

> issue interpretive guidance of the relevant rules of each chamber, including rules on conflicts of interest and gifts, clarifying that a Member of Congress and an employee of Congress may not use nonpublic information derived from such person's position as a Member of Congress or employee of Congress or gained from the performance of such person's official responsibilities as a means for making a private profit.[70]

On August 17, 2012, the committee issued a "pink sheet" on the implementation of the STOCK Act that clarified who is required to file, what transactions must be reported, the requirements for participating in a stock's initial public offering (IPO), waivers and exclusions to the act, when transactions must be reported, how and where transactions should be reported, late filing fees, penalties for failing to file and filing false information, and how to get assistance from the committee.[71]

Ethics Reform Act of 1989

The Ethics Reform Act of 1989 amended the Ethics in Government Act of 1978 and included a variety of ethics and pay reforms for the three branches of government. Enforcement of these changes further expanded the jurisdiction of the Committee on Ethics.[72]

Changes made pursuant to the Ethics Reform Act of 1989 included enforcement of the act's ban on honoraria, limits on outside earned income, and restrictions on the acceptance of gifts. The committee was also given the responsibility for consideration of any requests for a written waiver of the limits imposed by the House gift ban rule.[73]

PROCEDURES

Procedures for the Committee on Ethics are set through House Rule XI, clause 3 and are further specified in the committee's rules.[74]

Since its creation in 1967, several changes have been made to the Committee on Ethics' procedures. Change to the committee's procedures can be divided into six broad time periods or categories: changes in the 1970s, the Ethics Reform Act of 1989, the Ethics Reform Task Force of 1997, 109th Congress changes, 110th Congress changes, and the creation of the Office of Congressional Ethics in 2008.

Changes in the 1970s

During the first years of the Committee on Ethics many adjustments were made to the procedural operations of the committee. While some of the changes made during the 1970s have been repealed or replaced, three changes remain in effect.

1. In the 93rd Congress (1973-1974), the House agreed to H.Res. 988 and amended the jurisdiction and procedures of nearly all standing committees.[75] As part of those reforms, House Rules were amended to permit a majority vote to approve Committee on Standard's reports, recommendations, advisory opinions, and investigations;[76]
2. In the 95th Congress (1977-1978), the House included in its opening day rules package a provision permitting a member of the committee to disqualify himself/herself from participating in an investigation upon submission of an affidavit of disqualification in writing and under oath;[77] and
3. In the 96th Congress (1979-1980), House rules were amended to prohibit "information or testimony received, or the contents of a complaint or the fact of its filing" from being "publicly disclosed by any committee or staff member unless specifically authorized in each instance by a vote of the full committee."[78]

Ethics Reform Act of 1989

The Ethics Reform Act of 1989 (P.L. 101-194) contained provisions affecting all three branches of government and mandated changes to the House Committee on Ethics.[79] Specifically, it established the Office of Advice and Education in the Committee on Ethics. The Office of Advice and Education's primarily responsibilities include

a) Providing information and guidance to Members, officers and employees of the House regarding any laws, rules, regulations, and other standards of conduct applicable to such individuals in their official capacities, and any interpretations and advisory opinions of the committee.
b) Submitting to the chairman and ranking minority member of the committee any written request from any such Member, officer or employee for an interpretation of applicable laws, rules, regulations, or other standards of conduct, together with any recommendations thereon.
c) Recommending to the committee for its consideration formal advisory opinions of general applicability.
d) Developing and carrying out, subject to the approval of the chairman, periodic educational briefings for Members, officers and employees of the House on those laws, rules, regulations, or other standards of conduct applicable to them.[80]

The Office of Advice and Education offers training, guidance, and provides recommendations to Members, officers, and employees of the House on standards of conduct applicable to their official duties.[81]

Many other changes implemented by the 1989 act are still applicable. These include

- "bifurcation" (separation) within the committee of its investigative and adjudicative functions;[82]
- a requirement that the committee report to the House on any case it has voted to investigate and that any "letter of reproval" or other committee administrative action may be issued only as part of a final report to the House;[83]
- a statute of limitation prohibiting the committee from initiating or undertaking an investigation of alleged violations occurring prior to

the third previous Congress unless they are related to a continuous course of conduct in recent years;[84]

- a guarantee that any Member who is the respondent in any Ethics Committee investigation may be accompanied by one counsel on the House floor during consideration of his/her case;[85] and
- a time limit of committee service of no more than three out of any five consecutive Congresses.[86]

The act also increased the size of the committee's membership from 12 to 14.[87] That change, however, was superseded by the 1997 amendments that reduced the size of the committee from 14 to 10 members.[88]

Ethics Reform Task Force

On February 12, 1997, the House created an Ethics Reform Task Force to "look into any and all aspects of the ethics process," including:

> Who can file a complaint and upon what basis of information, what should be the standards for initiating an investigation, what evidentiary standard should apply throughout the process, how has the bifurcation process worked, does it take too long to conduct a review, should non-House Members play a part in a reformed ethics process, should we enlarge the pool of Members who might participate in different phases of the process?[89]

Chaired by Representatives Bob Livingston and Ben Cardin, the 10-member task force was directed to review the existing House ethics process and to recommend reforms.[90] At the same time that the House approved the establishment of the task force, it also approved a 65-day moratorium on the filing of new ethics complaints to enable the Task Force to conduct its work "in a climate free from specific questions of ethical propriety."[91]

After seven months of study, the Task Force reported to the House in June 1997 with several recommendations. These included ensuring that the Committee on Standards operated in a nonpartisan manner; that the committee's workings be kept confidential unless otherwise voted on by the committee; that an improved system be created for the filing of information offered as a complaint; that the committee should create an efficient administrative structure; that due process for Members, officers, and employees of the House be preserved; that Members play a greater role in the ethics process; and that matters before the committee be dealt with in a timely manner.[92] On September 18, 1997, the House debated and agreed to H.Res. 230, a rule to provide for the consideration of H.Res. 168, the implementation of the Task Force's recommendations,[93] and proceeded to debate and amend H.Res. 168.[94] The major ethics process changes adopted pursuant to H.Res. 168 included the following:

- altering the way individuals who are not Members of the House file complaints with the Committee on Ethics by requiring them to have a Member of the House certify in writing that the information is submitted in good faith and warrants consideration;[95]
- decreasing the size of the committee from 14 members to 10;[96]
- establishing a 20-person pool of Members (10 from each party) to supplement the work of the Ethics Committee as potential appointees to investigative subcommittees that the committee might establish; [97]
- requiring the chair and ranking minority member of the committee to determine within 14 calendar days or 5 legislative days, whichever comes first, if the information offered as a complaint meets the committee's requirements;[98]
- allowing an affirmative vote of two-thirds of the members of the committee or approval of the full House to refer evidence of violations of law disclosed in a committee investigation to the appropriate state or federal law enforcement authorities;[99]
- providing for a nonpartisan, professional committee staff;[100]
- allowing the ranking minority member on the committee to place matters on the committee's agenda;[101] and
- decreasing the maximum service on the committee from six years to four years during any three successive Congresses and required at least four members to be rotated off the committee at the end of each Congress.[102]

109th Congress Changes

On January 4, 2005, the House included several provisions in its rules for the 109th Congress (2005-2006) that affected the Committee on Ethics. These included the process for handling allegations against a House Member, officer, or employee; procedures for instances when the conduct of one Member, officer, or employee might be referenced in the course of an investigation against another Member, officer, or employee; the due process for respondents and witnesses; and the dismissal of complaints.[103]

Subsequently, on April 27, 2005, the House reversed earlier 109th Congress changes when it agreed to H.Res. 240 and reinstated "certain provisions of the rules relating to procedures of the Committee on Standards of Official Conduct to the form in which those provisions existed at the close of the 108th Congress."[104]

110th Congress Changes

On June 5, 2007, the House agreed to H.Res. 451, directing the Committee on Ethics to "respond to the indictment of, or the filing of charges of criminal conduct in a court of the United States or any State against, any Member of the House of Representatives by empanelling an investigative subcommittee to review the allegations not later than 30 days after the date the Member is indicted or the charges are filed."[105] The resolution was adopted following the grand jury indictment of a Member of the House in the United States District Court for the Eastern District of Virginia. The requirements of H.Res. 451 were continued in the rules packages for both the 111th and the 112th Congresses.[106]

113th Congress Changes

As part of the rules package (H.Res. 5) for the 113th Congress (2013-2014), the House amended the Code of Conduct (Rule XXIII, clause 8(c)) to remove references to "spouses" and replace those references with the term "relative." For the purpose of the Rule, relative is defined as

> an individual who is related to the Member, Delegate, or Resident Commissioner as father, mother, son, daughter, brother, sister, uncle, aunt, first cousin, nephew, niece, husband, wife, father-in-law, mother-in-law, son-in-law, daughter-in-law, brother-in-law, sister-in-law, stepfather, stepmother, stepson, stepdaughter, stepbrother, stepsister, half brother, half sister, grandson, or granddaughter.[107]

Additionally, H.Res. 5 required that copies of executed oaths (or affirmations) made by an officer or employee of the House be retained by the Sergeant at Arms, while oaths (or affirmations) made by Members, Delegates, or the Resident Commissioner continue to be retained by the Clerk of the House.[108]

Office of Congressional Ethics

In January 2007, Speaker of the House Nancy Pelosi and Minority Leader John Boehner jointly established a Special Task Force on Ethics Enforcement in the House of Representatives.[109] Chaired by Representative Michael Capuano, the task force was charged with considering "whether the House should create an outside enforcement entity, based on examples in state legislatures and private entities."[110]

In December 2007, Chairman Capuano released a report and introduced H.Res. 895 to create an office of congressional ethics, composed of six board members jointly appointed by House leaders.[111] On March 11, 2008, the House adopted H.Res. 895 and created the Office of Congressional Ethics (OCE).[112]

The first OCE board members were appointed in July 2008.[113] The OCE held its first public meeting on January 23, 2009, and began to implement the structural requirements of H.Res. 895. It also adopted rules of procedure, a code of conduct, and rules for the conduct of a review. The Office of Congressional Ethics (OCE) was reauthorized by the House as part of the rules package (H.Res. 5) adopted by the 113th Congress on January 3, 2013.[114]

APPENDIX. MEMBERSHIP ON THE COMMITTEE ON ETHICS, 1967-2013

Since its inception in the 90th Congress (1967-1968), the Committee on Ethics has had a total of 284 members.[115] *Table A-1* provides a list of all Members to have served on the Committee on Ethics, their party affiliation, and their state and district.

Table A-1. Congressional Committee Assignments: House Committee on Ethics

Member	Party	State	District
	90th Congress (1967-1968)		
Price, C. Melvin	D	IL	24th
Teague, Olin E.	D	T)(	6th
Evins, Joseph L.	D	TN	4th
Abbitt, Watkins M.	D	VA	4th
Aspinall, Wayne N.	D	CO	4th
Kelly, Edna F.	D	NY	12th
Halleck, Charles A.	R	IN	2nd
Arends, Leslie C.	R	IL	17th
Betts, Jackson E.	R	OH	8th
Stafford, Robert T.	R	VT	AL [a]
Quillen, James H.	R	TN	1st
Williams, Lawrence G.	R	PA	7th
	91st Congress (1969-1970)		
Price, C. Melvin	D	IL	24th
Teague, Olin E.	D	T)(	6th
Abbitt, Watkins M.	D	VA	4th
Aspinall, Wayne N.	D	CO	4th
Hébert, F. Edward	D	LA	1st
Holifield, Chet	D	CA	19th
Arends, Leslie C.	R	IL	17th
Betts, Jackson E.	R	OH	8th
Stafford, Robert T.	R	VT	AL [a]
Quillen, James H.	R	TN	1st
Williams, Lawrence G.	R	PA	7th
Hutchinson, Edward	R	MI	4th
Reid, Charlotte T.	R	IL	15th
	92nd Congress (1971-1972)		
Price, C. Melvin	D	IL	24th
Teague, Olin E.	D	TX	6th
Abbitt, Watkins M.	D	VA	4th
Aspinall, Wayne N.	D	CO	4th
Hébert, F. Edward	D	LA	1st
Holifield, Chet	D	CA	19th
Betts, Jackson E.	R	OH	8th
Stafford, Robert T.	R	VT	AL [a]
Quillen, James H.	R	TN	1st
Williams, Lawrence G.	R	PA	7th
Hutchinson, Edward	R	MI	4th

Table A-1. (Continued)

Member	Party	State	District
Reid, Charlotte T.	R	IL	15th
King, Carleton J.	R	NY	30th
Spence, Floyd D.	R	SC	2nd
	93rd Congress (1973-1974)		
Price, C. Melvin	D	IL	23rd
Teague, Olin E.	D	TX	6th
Hébert, F. Edward	D	LA	1st
Holifield, Chet	D	CA	19th
Flynt, John James Jr.	D	GA	6th
Foley, Thomas S.	D	WA	5th
Quillen, James H.	R	TN	1st
Williams, Lawrence G.	R	PA	7th
Hutchinson, Edward	R	MI	4th
King, Carleton J.	R	NY	29th
Spence, Floyd D.	R	SC	2nd
Hunt, John E.	R	NJ	1st
	94th Congress (1975-1976)		
Price, C. Melvin	D	IL	23
Teague, Olin E.	D	TX	6th
Hébert, F. Edward	D	LA	1st
Flynt, John James Jr.	D	GA	6th
Foley, Thomas S.	D	WA	5th
Bennett, Charles E.	D	FL	3rd
Spence, Floyd D.	R	SC	2nd
Quillen, James H.	R	TN	1st
Hutchinson, Edward	R	MI	4th
Quie, Albert H.	R	MN	1st
Mitchell, Donald J.	R	NY	31st
Cochran, Thad	R	MS	4th
	95th Congress (1977-1978)		
Flynt, John James Jr.	D	GA	6th
Teague, Olin E.	D	TX	6th
Bennett, Charles E	D	FL	3rd
Hamilton, Lee H.	D	IN	9th

Member	Party	State	District
Preyer, L. Richardson	D	NC	6th
Flowers, Walter	D	AL	7th
Spence, Floyd D.	R	SC	2nd
Quillen, James H.	R	TN	1st
Quie, Albert H.	R	MN	1st
Cochran, Thad	R	MS	4th
Fenwick, Millicent H.	R	NJ	5th
Caputo, Bruce F.	R	NY	23
	96th Congress (1979-1980)		
Bennett, Charles E.	D	FL	3rd
Hamilton, Lee H.	D	IN	9th
Preyer, L. Richardson	D	NC	6th
Slack, John M. Jr.	D	WV	3rd
Murphy, Morgan F.	D	IL	2nd
Murtha, John P. Jr.	D	PA	12th
Spence, Floyd D.	R	SC	2nd
Hollenbeck, Harold C.	R	NJ	9th
Livingston, Robert L.	R	LA	1st
Thomas, William M.	R	CA	18th
Sensenbrenner, F. James Jr.	R	WI	9th
Cheney, Richard B.	R	WY	AL [a]
Stokes, Louis	D	OH	21st
Rahall, Nick J. II	D	WV	4th
	97th Congress (1981-1982)		
Stokes, Louis	D	OH	21st
Rahall, Nick J. II	D	WV	4th
Alexander, William V. Jr.	D	AR	1st
Wilson, Charles	D	TX	2nd
Holland, Kenneth L.	D	SC	5th
Bailey, Donald A.	D	PA	21st
Spence, Floyd d.	R	SC	2nd
Conable, Barber B. Jr.	R	NY	35th
Myers, John T.	R	IN	7th
Forsythe, Edwin B.	R	NJ	6th

Table A-1. (Continued)

Member	Party	State	District
Brown, Hank	R	CO	4th
Hansen, James V.	R	UT	1st
	98th Congress (1983-1984)		
Stokes, Louis	D	OH	21st
Rahall, Nick J. II	D	WV	4th
Jenkins, Edgar L.	D	GA	9th
Dixon, Julian C.	D	CA	28th
Fazio, Victor H.	D	CA	4th
Coyne, William J.	D	PA	14th
Spence, Floyd D.	R	SC	2nd
Conable, Barber B. Jr.	R	NY	30th
Myers, John T.	R	IN	7th
Forsythe, Edwin B.	R	NJ	13th
Brown, Hank	R	CO	4th
Hansen, James V.	R	UT	1st
Bliley, Thomas J. Jr.	R	VA	3rd
	99th Congress (1985-1986)		
Dixon, Julian C.	D	CA	28th
Jenkins, Edgar L.	D	GA	9th
Fazio, Victor H.	D	CA	4th
Coyne, William J.	D	PA	14th
Dwyer, Bernard J.	D	NJ	6th
Mollohan, Alan B.	D	WV	1st
Spence, Floyd D.	R	SC	2nd
Myers, John T.	R	IN	7th
Hansen, James V.	R	UT	1st
Whitehurst, G. William	R	VA	2nd
Pursell, Carl D.	R	MI	2nd
Wortley, George	R	NY	27th
	100th Congress (1987-1988)		
Dixon, Julian C.	D	CA	28th
Fazio, Victor H.	D	CA	4th
Dwyer, Bernard J.	D	NJ	6th
Mollohan, Alan B.	D	WV	1st

Member	Party	State	District
Gaydos, Joseph M.	D	PA	20th
Atkins, Chester G.	D	MA	5th
Spence, Floyd	R	SC	2nd
Myers, John T.	R	IN	7th
Hansen, James V.	R	UT	1st
Pashayan, Charles S. Jr.	R	CA	17th
Petri, Thomas E.	R	WI	6th
Craig, Larry E.	R	ID	1st
Brown, Hank	R	CO	4th
	101st Congress (1989-1990)		
Dixon, Julian C.	D	CA	29th
Fazio, Victor H.	D	CA	4th
Dwyer, Bernard J.	D	CA	29th
Mollohan, Alan B.	D	NJ	6th
Gaydos, Joseph M.	D	WV	1st
Atkins, Chester G.	D	PA	20th
Stokes, Louis [b]	D	OH	21st
Myers, John T.	R	IN	7th
Hansen, James V.	R	UT	1st
Pashayan, Charles S. Jr.	R	CA	17th
Petri, Thomas E.	R	WI	6th
Craig, Larry E.	R	ID	1st
Grandy, Fred	R	IA	6th
	102nd Congress (1991-1992)		
Stokes, Louis	D	OH	21st
Ackerman, Gary L.	D	NY	7th
Darden, George (Buddy)	D	GA	7th
Cardin, Benjamin L.	D	MD	3rd
Pelosi, Nancy	D	CA	5th
McDermott, Jim	D	WA	7th
Mfume, Kweisi [c]	D	MD	7th
Hansen, James V.	R	UT	1st
Grandy, Fred	R	IA	6th
Johnson, Nancy L.	R	CT	6th
Bunning, Jim	R	KY	4th
Kyl, Jon L.	R	AZ	4th

Table A-1. (Continued)

Member	Party	State	District
Goss, Porter J.	R	FL	13th
Hobson, David L.	R	OH	7th
	103rd Congress (1993-1994)		
McDermott, Jim	D	WA	7th
Darden, George (Buddy)	D	GA	7th
Cardin, Benjamim L.	D	MD	3rd
Pelosi, Nancy	D	CA	5th
Mfume, Kweisi	D	MD	7th
Borski, Robert A.	D	PA	3rd
Sawyer, Thomas C.	D	OH	14th
Grandy, Fred	R	IA	6th
Johnson, Nancy L.	R	CT	6th
Bunning, Jim	R	KY	4th
Kyl, Jon L.	R	AZ	4th
Goss, Porter J.	R	FL	13th
Hobson, David L.	R	OH	7th
Schiff, Steven	R	NY	1st
	104th Congress (1995-1996)[d]		
Johnson, Nancy L.	R	CT	6th
Bunning, Jim	R	KY	4th
Goss, Porter J.	R	FL	13th
Hobson, David L.	R	OH	7th
Schiff, Steven	R	NM	1st
Smith, Lamar S. [e]	R	TX	21st
McDermott, Jim [f]	D	WA	7th
Cardin, Benjamin L.	D	MD	3rd
Pelosi, Nancy	D	CA	5th
Borski, Robert A.	D	PA	3rd
Sawyer, Thomas C.	D	OH	14th
	105th Congress (1997-1998)		
Hansen, James V.	R	UT	1st
Smith, Lamar S.	R	TX	21st
Hefley, Joel	R	CO	5th
Goodlatte, Robert	R	VA	6th
Knollenberg, Joe	R	MI	11th

Member	Party	State	District
Berman, Howard L.	D	CA	26th
Sabo, Martin O.	D	MN	5th
Pastor, Ed	D	AZ	2nd
Fattah, Chaka	D	PA	2nd
Lofgren, Zoe	D	CA	16th
	106th Congress (1999-2000)		
Smith, Lamar S.	R	TX	21st
Hefley, Joel	R	CO	5th
Knollenberg, Joe	R	MI	11th
Portman, Robert J.	R	OH	2nd
Camp, Dave	R	MI	4th
Berman, Howard L.	D	CA	26th
Sabo, Martin O.	D	MN	5th
Pastor, Ed	D	AZ	2nd
Fattah, Chaka	D	PA	2nd
Lofgren, Zoe	D	CA	16th
	107th Congress (2001-2002)		
Hefley, Joel	R	CO	5th
Portman, Robert J.	R	OH	2nd
Hastings, Doc	R	WA	4th
Hutchison, Asa	R	AR	3rd
Biggert, Judy	R	IL	13th
Hulshof, Kenny	R	MO	9th
LaTourette, Steve	R	OH	19th
Berman, Howard	D	CA	26th
Sabo, Martin O.	D	MN	5th
Pastor, Ed	D	AZ	2nd
Lofgren, Zoe	D	CA	16th
Jones, Stephanie Tubbs	D	OH	11th
Green, Gene	D	TX	29th
	108th Congress (2003-2004)		
Hefley, Joel	R	CO	5th
Hastings, Doc	R	WA	4th
Biggert, Judy	R	IL	13th
Hulshof, Kenny	R	MO	9th
LaTourette, Steve	R	OH	19th
Berman, Howard	D	CA	26th
Mollohan, Alan B.	D	WV	1st
Jones, Stephanie Tubbs	D	OH	11th
Green, Gene	D	TX	29th
Roybal-Allard, Lucille	D	CA	34th
Doyle, Michael F.	D	PA	14th

Table A-1. (Continued)

Member	Party	State	District
	109th Congress (2005-2006)		
Hastings, Doc	R	WA	4th
Biggert, Judy	R	IL	13th
Smith, Lamar S.	R	TX	21st
Hart, Melissa	R	TX	4th
Cole, Tom	R	OK	4th
Mollohan, Alan B.	D	WV	1st
Berman, Howard, L. [g]	D	CA	28th
Jones, Stephanie Tubbs	D	OH	11th
Green, Gene	D	TX	29th
Roybal-Allard, Lucille	D	CA	34th
Doyle, Michael F.	D	PA	14th
	110th Congress (2007-2008)		
Jones, Stephanie Tubbsh	D	OH	11th
Green, Gene	D	TX	29th
Roybal-Allard, Lucille	D	CA	34th
Doyle, Michael F.	D	PA	14th
Delahunt, William D.	D	MA	10th
Scott, Robert C. "Bobby"	D	VA	3rd
Hastings, Doc	R	WA	4th
Bonner, Jo	R	AL	1st
Barrett, J. Gresham	R	SC	3rd
Kline, John	R	MN	2nd
McCaul, Michael T.	R	TX	10th
	111th Congress (2009-2010)		
Lofgren, Zoe	D	CA	16th
Chandler, Ben	D	KY	6th
Butterfield, G.K.	D	NC	1st
Castor, Kathy	D	FL	11th
Welch, Peter	D	VT	AL [a]
Bonner, Jo	R	AL	1st
Conaway, K. Michael	R	TX	11th
Dent, Charles W.	R	PA	15th
Harper, Gregg	R	MS	3rd
McCaul, Michael T.	R	TX	10th
	112th Congress (2011-2012)		
Bonner, Jo	R	AL	1st
McCaul, Michael T.	R	TX	10th
Conaway, K. Michael	R	TX	11th
Dent, Charles W.	R	PA	15th

Member	Party	State	District
Harper, Gregg	R	MS	3rd
Lofgren, Zoe [i]	D	CA	16th
Sánchez, Linda	D	CA	39th
Hirono, Mazie [j]	D	HI	2nd
Yarmuth, John	D	KY	3rd
Edwards, Donna	D	MD	4th
Pierluisi, Pedro	D	PR	AL [k]
Courtney, Joe [l]	D	CT	2nd
	113th Congress (2013-2014)		
Conaway, K. Michael	R	TX	11th
Dent, Charles W.	R	PA	15th
Meehan, Patrick	R	PA	7th
Gowdy, Trey	R	SC	4th
Brooks, Susan	R	IN	5th
Sánchez, Linda T.	D	CA	39th
Pierluisi, Pedro	D	PR	AL
Capuano, Michael E.	D	MA	7th
Clarke, Yvette D.	D	NY	9th
Deutch, Ted	D	FL	21st

Source: Garrison Nelson, Mary T. Mitchell, and Clark H. Bensen, Committees in the U.S. Congress: 1947-1992 (Washington: CQ Press, 1994); U.S. Congress, Joint Committee on Printing, 1993-1994 Official Congressional Directory: 103rd Congress, 103rd Cong., 1st sess., S.Pub. 103-8 (Washington: GPO, 1994), p. 471; U.S. Congress, Joint Committee on Printing, 1995-1996 Official Congressional Directory: 104th Congress, 104th Cong., 1st sess., S.Pub. 104-14 (Washington: GPO, 1996), p. 417; U.S. Congress, Joint Committee on Printing, 1997-1998 Official Congressional Directory: 105th Congress, 105th Cong., 1st sess., S.Pub. 105-20 (Washington: GPO, 1998), p. 439; U.S. Congress, Joint Committee on Printing, 1999-2000 Official Congressional Directory: 106th Congress, 106th Cong., 1st sess., S.Pub. 106-21 (Washington: GPO, 2000), p. 423; U.S. Congress, Joint Committee on Printing, 2001-2002 Official Congressional Directory: 107th Congress, 107th Cong., 1st sess., S.Pub. 107-20 (Washington: GPO, 2002), p. 430; U.S. Congress, Joint Committee on Printing, 2003-2004 Official Congressional Directory: 108th Congress, 108th Cong., 1st sess., S.Pub. 108-18 (Washington: GPO, 2004), p. 425; U.S. Congress, Joint Committee on Printing, 2005-2006 Official Congressional Directory: 109th Congress, 109th Cong., 1st sess., S.Pub. 109-12 (Washington: GPO, 2006), p. 434; U.S. Congress, Joint Committee on Printing, 2007-2008 Official Congressional Directory: 110th Congress, 110th Cong., 1st sess., S.Pub. 110-13 (Washington: GPO, 2008), p. 432; U.S. Congress, Joint Committee on Printing, 2009-2010 Official Congressional Directory: 111th Congress, 111th Cong., 1st sess., S.Pub. 111-14 (Washington: GPO, 2010), p. 444; H.Res. 6 and H.Res. 7 (113th Congress), agreed to January 3, 2013 ("Electing Members to Certain Standing Committees of the House of Representatives," Congressional Record, daily edition, vol. 159 (January 3, 2013), p. H23); and "Electing Members to Certain Standing Committees of the House of Representatives," Congressional Record, daily edition, vol. 159 (January 23, 2013), p. H250.

Notes:

[a] Representative at Large (i.e., the state's only Member of the House of Representatives).

[b] Appointed to replace Representative Chester G. Atkins.

[c] Appointed to replace Representative Louis Stokes and Representative Gary L. Ackerman.

[d] Most of the Members of the committee from the 104th Congress were appointed to the Select Committee on Ethics in the 105th Congress, which existed from January 7, 1997 to January 21, 1997. This select committee was established to resolve the Statement of Alleged Violations issued in the 104th Congress by the Committee on Standards of Official Conduct against the Speaker of the House. This select committee expired on January 21, 1997, with the House approving a reprimand against Speaker Newt Gingrich.

e Appointed to the Select Committee on Ethics to complete the investigation begun by the Committee of Standards of Official Conduct.

f Representative McDermott was briefly replaced (July 23 to July 24, 1996) by Representative Louis Stokes (D-OH) during a committee inquiry involving Representative McDermott.

g Representative Berman was appointed as ranking member after Representative Mollohan's resignation.

h Representative Tubbs-Jones died on August 20, 2008. Representative Gene Green served as acting chair for the remainder of the 110th Congress.

i Representative Lofgren resigned as ranking member on January 26, 2011 ["Resignation as a Member of the Committee on Ethics," Congressional Record, daily edition, vol. 157 (January 26, 2011), p. H499].

j Representative Hirono resigned from the committee on July 14, 2011 ["Resignation as Member of Committee on Ethics," Congressional Record, daily edition, vol. 157 (July 14, 2011), p. H5050].

k Resident Commissioner Pierluisi represents the Commonwealth of Puerto Rico in the House and is the first Ethics Committee member who represents a territory. For more information on the Resident Commissioner, see CRS Report RL31856, Resident Commissioner from Puerto Rico, by R. Eric Petersen.

l Representative Courtney was appointed to the committee on July 14, 2011 ["Electing a Member to a Certain Standing Committee of the House of Representatives," Congressional Record, daily edition, vol. 157 (July 14, 2011), p. H5050].

End Notes

[1] James Madison, "Federalist No. 57, The Alleged Tendency of the New Plan to Elevate the Few at the Expense of the Many Considered in Connection with Representation," The Federalist Papers, February 19, 1788, from the New York Packet, http://thomas.loc.gov/home/histdox/fed_57.html.

[2] U.S. Congress, "Article I, Section 5, clause 2," The Constitution of the United States, 108th Cong., 1st sess., H.Doc. 108-96 (Washington: GPO, 2003), p. 4.

[3] Ibid.

[4] U.S. Congress, Committee on House Administration, History of the United States House of Representatives, 1789- 1994, 103rd Cong., 2nd sess., H.Doc. 103-324 (Washington: GPO, 1994), p. 293.

[5] Richard Baker, "The History of Congressional Ethics," in Bruce Jennings and Daniel Callahan, eds., Representation and Responsibility: Exploring Legislative Ethics (New York: Plenum Press, 1985), p. 4. [Hereafter, Baker, "The History of Congressional Ethics"].

[6] Baker, "The History of Congressional Ethics," p. 3.

[7] U.S. Congress, House, Select Committee Pursuant to House Resolution 1, In Re Adam Clayton Powell, report to accompany H.Res. 278, 90th Cong., 1st sess., February 23, 1967, H.Rept. 90-27 (Washington: GPO, 1967); and Powell v. McCormick, 395 U.S. 486 (1969).

[8] Robert V. Remini, The House: The History of the House of Representatives (Washington: Smithsonian Books, 2006), p. 414.

[9] For more information on Members indicted or convicted of a felony, see CRS Report RL33229, Status of a Member of the House Who Has Been Indicted for or Convicted of a Felony, by Jack Maskell. For more information on the enforcement of codes of Conduct in the House of Representatives and the Senate, see CRS Report RL30764, Enforcement of Congressional Rules of Conduct: An Historical Overview, by Jacob R. Straus.

[10] 72 Stat. B12, H.Con.Res. 175, July 11, 1958. See also "Code of Ethics For Government Service," House proceeding, Congressional Record, vol. 103, part 12 (August 28, 1957), p. 16297; and "Code of Ethics For Government Service," Senate proceeding, Congressional Record, vol. 104, part 10 (July 11, 1958), p. 13556.

[11] Rep. Charles Bennett, "Code of Ethics for Government Service," remarks in the House, Congressional Record, vol. 97, part 5 (June 26, 1951), pp. 7176-7178; and Testimony of Rep. Charles Bennett, in U.S. Congress, House Committee on Post Office and Civil Service, Code of Ethics For Government Service, hearings, 84th Cong., 2nd sess., March 29, 1956 (Washington: GPO, 1956), pp. 3-5.

[12] Because the code was adopted by concurrent resolution rather than statute, it does not have the force of law and technically expired at the end of the Congress adopting it. The Code of Ethics for Government Service is, however, cited by many House and Senate investigations. For example, see U.S. Congress, House, Committee on Standards of Official Conduct, Investigation of Certain Allegations Related to Voting on the Medicare Prescription Drug, Improvement, and Modernization Act of 2003, report, 108th Cong., 2nd sess., H.Rept. 108-722 (Washington: GPO, 2004), p. 38; and U. S. Congress, Senate Select Committee on Ethics, Korean Influence Investigation, report, 95th Cong., 2nd sess., S. Rept. 95-1314 (Washington: GPO, 1975), pp. 5-6.

[13] Baker, "The History of Congressional Ethics," p. 4.

[14] "Ethics," in Congress and the Nation, 1945-1964 (Washington: Congressional Quarterly Inc., 1965), p. 1409.

[15] U.S. Congress, Joint Committee on the Organization of Congress, Index to Hearings Before the Joint Committee on the Organization of Congress, pursuant to S.Res. 2, 89th Cong, 1st and 2nd sess., various dates 1965 and 1966, part 16 (Washington: GPO, 1966), p. 45.

[16] U.S. Congress, Joint Committee on the Organization of Congress, Organization of Congress, final report pursuant to S.Res. 2, 89th Cong., 2nd sess., S.Rept. 89-1414 (Washington: GPO, 1966), p. 48.

[17] "Public Bills and Resolutions," Congressional Record, vol. 112, part 16 (September 2, 1966), p. 21738.

[18] U.S. Congress, House, Committee on Rules, Creating a Select Committee on Standards and Conduct, report to accompany H.Res. 1013, 89th Cong., 2nd sess., September 7, 1966, H.Rept. 89-2012 (Washington: GPO, 1966); and Rep. Claude Pepper, "Creating a Select Committee on Standards and Conduct," remarks in the House, Congressional Record, vol. 112, part 16 (September 7, 1966), p. 21949.

[19] "Creating a Select Committee on Standards and Conduct," House debate, Congressional Record, vol. 112, part 20 (October 19, 1966), pp. 27713-27730.

[20] U.S. Congress, House, Select Committee on Standards and Conduct, Report of the Select Committee on Standards and Conduct of the House of Representatives, under the authority of H.Res. 1013, 89th Cong., 2nd sess., December 27, 1966, H.Rept. 89-2338 (Washington: GPO, 1966), p. vii.

[21] U.S. Congress, House, Select Committee on Standards and Conduct, Report Under the Authority of H.Res. 1013, 89th Cong., 2nd sess., H.Rept. 89-2338 (Washington: GPO, 1966), p. 1.

[22] Ibid.

[23] "Public Bills and Resolutions," Congressional Record, vol. 113, part 1 (January 10, 1967), p. 130.

[24] U.S. Congress, House, Committee on Rules, Creating a Select Committee on Standards and Conduct, hearing on H.Res. 18 and Similar Measures, 90th Cong., 1st sess., February 21 and 22, 1967 (Washington: GPO, 1967); U.S. Congress, House Committee on Rules, Creating a Select Committee on Standards and Conduct: Part 2, hearing on H.Res. 18 and similar measures, 90th Cong., 1st sess., February 28, 1967 (Washington: GPO, 1967); and U.S. Congress, House Committee on Rules, Creating a Select Committee on Standards and Conduct: Part 3, hearings on H.Res. 18 and similar measures, 90th Cong., 1st sess., March 7, 8, 14, and 15, 1967 (Washington: GPO, 1967).

[25] U.S. Congress, House, Committee on Rules, Creating a Select Committee on Standards and Conduct, hearing on H.Res. 18 and Similar Measures, 90th Cong., 1st sess., February 21 and 22, 1967 (Washington: GPO, 1967), p 8.

[26] U.S. Congress, House, Committee on Rules, Establishing a Standing Committee to be Known as the Committee on Standards of Official Conduct, and for Other Purposes, report to accompany H.Res. 418, 90th Cong., 1st sess., April 6, 1967, H.Rept. 90-178 (Washington: GPO, 1967). For more information on the Committee on Rules ability to issue privileged reports in the 90th Congress, see Rule XI, clause 22 (90th Congress) in U.S. Congress, House, Constitution, Jefferson's Manual, and Rules of the House of Representatives of the United States Ninetieth Congress, prepared by Lewis Deschler, Parliamentarian, 89th Cong., 2nd sess. (Washington: GPO, 1967), pp. 360-361.

[27] Rep. William Colmer, "To Establish a Standing Committee to be Known as the Committee on Standards of Official Conduct, and for Other Purposes," Congressional Record, vol. 113, part 7 (April 6, 1967), p. 8622; and Rep. William Colmer, "Establishing a Standing

Committee on Standards and Conduct," Journal of the House of Representatives of the United States, 90th cong., 1st sess., (April 6, 1967), p. 463.

[28] "Committee on Standards of Official Conduct," House debate, Congressional Record, vol. 113, part 7 (April 13, 1967), pp. 9426-9448.

[29] Ibid., p. 9426.

[30] "Committee on Standards of Official Conduct," Journal of the House of Representatives of the United States, 90th cong., 1st sess., (April 13, 1967), p. 488.

[31] Rep. Wilber Mills, "Election to Committee—Majority," Journal of the House of Representatives of the United States, 90th cong., 1st sess. (May 1, 1967), p. 539. The majority committee members were Representatives Melvin Price (chair), Olin Teague, Joe Evins, Watkins Abbitt, Wayne Aspinall, and Edna Kelly.

[32] Rep. Gerald Ford, "Election to Committee—Minority," Journal of the House of Representatives of the United States, 90th cong., 1st sess. (May 1, 1967), p. 539. The minority committee members were Representatives Charles Halleck, Leslie Arends, Jackson Betts, Robert Stafford, James Quillen, and Lawrence Williams.

[33] U.S. Congress, House, Committee on Standards of Official Conduct, Standards of Official Conduct, hearings, 90th Cong., 1st sess., August 16-17, 23-24, and September 14, 21, and 27, 1967 (Washington: GPO, 1967).

[34] Ibid., p. 1.

[35] The Corrupt Practices Act (P.L. 61-274, 36 Stat. 822, June 25, 1910) was repealed by the Federal Election Campaign Act in 1971 (P.L. 92-225, 86 Stat. 3, February 7, 1972; 2 U.S.C. §431 et seq., as amended). For more information on the Federal Election Campaign Act, see CRS Report R41542, The State of Campaign Finance Policy: Recent Developments and Issues for Congress, by R. Sam Garrett.

[36] U.S. Congress, House, Committee on Standards of Official Conduct, Code of Conduct for Members and Employees of the House, report under the authority of H.Res. 418, 90th Cong., 2nd sess., H.Rept. 90-1176 (Washington: GPO, 1968), pp. 7-11.

[37] "Public Bills and Resolutions," Congressional Record, vol. 114, part 5 (March 14, 1968), p. 6503.

[38] U.S. Congress, House, Committee on Rules, Amending H.Res. 418, 90th Congress, to Continue the Committee on Standards of Official Conduct as a Permanent Standing Committee of the House of Representatives, and for Other Purposes, report to accompany H.Res. 1099, 90th Cong., 2nd sess., H.Rept. 90-1248 (Washington: GPO, 1968). See also "Reports of Committees on Public Bills and Resolutions," Congressional Record, vol. 114, part 7 (April 1, 1968), p. 8406.

[39] Rep. Melvin Price, "Standards of Official Conduct," House debate, Congressional Record, vol. 114, part 7 (April 3, 1968), p. 8778.

[40] Ibid., p. 8812.

[41] Rule XLIII is currently codified as Rule XXIII. For the original text of the Code of Official Conduct, see U.S. Congress, House, Constitution, Jefferson's Manual, and Rules of the House of Representatives of the United States Ninety-First Congress, Lewis Deschler, Parliamentarian, 90th Cong., 2nd sess., H.Doc. 90-402 (Washington: GPO, 1969), pp. 499a-499b. For current Code of Official Conduct language, see U.S. Congress, House, Constitution, Jefferson's Manual, and Rules of the House of Representatives One Hundred Eleventh Congress of the United States, John V. Sullivan, Parliamentarian, 110th Cong., 2nd sess., H.Doc. 110-162 (Washington: GPO, 2003), pp. 918-928; and CRS Report RL30764, Enforcement of Congressional Rules of Conduct: An Historical Overview, by Jacob R. Straus.

[42] H.Res. 1099 (90th Congress), agreed to April 3, 1968. Rule XLIV is currently codified as Rule XXVI. For the original text of Financial Disclosure requirements, see U.S. Congress, House, Constitution, Jefferson's Manual, and Rules of the House of Representatives of the United States Ninety-First Congress, Lewis Deschler, Parliamentarian, 90th Cong., 2nd sess., H.Doc. 90-402 (Washington: GPO, 1969), pp. 499c-499f. For current Code of Official Conduct language, see U.S. Congress, House, Constitution, Jefferson's Manual, and Rules of the House of Representatives One Hundred Eleventh Congress of the United States, John V. Sullivan, Parliamentarian, 110th Cong., 2nd sess., H.Doc. 110- 162 (Washington: GPO, 2003), pp. 962-986.

[43] H.Res. 5 (112th Congress), agreed to January 5, 2011; "Rules of the House" Congressional Record, daily edition, vol. 157 (January 5, 2011), p. H7.

[44] With the adoption of H.Res. 168 (105th Congress) on September 18, 1997, the House voted to permit an affirmative vote of two-thirds of the full Standards Committee or the approval of the House for the referral of evidence of violations of law to the appropriate law enforcement authorities.

[45] U.S. Congress, Committee on House Administration, History of the United States House of Representatives, 1789- 1994, 103rd Cong., 2nd sess., H.Doc. 103-324 (Washington: GPO, 1994), p. 298.

[46] Ibid.

[47] The seven Member requirement was replaced in 1974 with "an affirmative vote by a majority of the members of the committee" to accommodate any subsequent changes in the committee's size (H.Res. 998, agreed to October 8, 1974). In 1991, pursuant to the Ethics Reform Act of 1989, the membership was increased to 14. However, in 1997, with the adoption of the recommendation of the Ethics Reform Task Force (H.Res. 168), the membership was reduced to 10. Also in the 105th Congress (1997-1999), the House permitted the chair and ranking minority member to gather additional information or establish an investigative subcommittee for a properly filed complaint (H.Res. 168, Section 11, agreed to September 18, 1997).

[48] H.Res. 168 (105th Congress), agreed to September 18, 1997, changed the requirements for the filing of complaints by non-Members to require that such complaints be transmitted by a Member who "certifies in writing to the committee that he or she believes the information is submitted in good faith and warrants the review and consideration of the Committee."

[49] This rule was expanded by the Ethics Reform Act of 1989 to include a statute of limitations of three previous Congresses for investigations of alleged violations (P.L. 101-194, Section 803(g), 103 Stat. 1775, November 30, 1989).

[50] Committee rule 9, clauses (d) and (e) require that a committee Member under investigation or who has a conflict of interest with an investigation be excluded from those proceedings. The rule states: "(d) A member of the Committee shall be ineligible to participate in any Committee or subcommittee proceeding in which such Member is the respondent;" and "(e) A member of the Committee may seek disqualification from participating in any investigation of the conduct of a Member, officer, or employee of the House of Representatives upon the submission in writing and under oath of an affidavit of disqualification stating that the member cannot render an impartial and unbiased decision. If the Committee approves and accepts such affidavit of disqualification, the Chair shall so notify the Speaker and ask the Speaker to designate a Member of the House of Representatives from the same political party as the disqualified member of the Committee to act as a member of the Committee in any Committee proceeding relating to such investigation" (U.S. Congress, House, Committee on Standards of Official Conduct, Rules,

111th Cong., 1st sess., June 9, 2009 (http://ethics.house.gov/Media/PDF/111th_Rules_Amended_June_2009.pdf), pp. 16-17.

[51] U.S. Congress, Committee on House Administration, History of the United States House of Representatives, 1789- 1994, 103rd Cong., 2nd sess., H.Doc. 103-324 (Washington: GPO, 1994), p. 298.

[52] For more information on the Parliamentarian of the House and the referral process, see CRS Report RS20544, The Office of the Parliamentarian in the House and Senate, by Valerie Heitshusen and CRS Report 98-175, House Committee Jurisdiction and Referral: Rules and Practice, by Judy Schneider.

[53] U.S. Congress, House, Committee on Standards of Official Conduct, House Ethics Manual: 2008 Edition, 110th Cong., 2nd sess. (Washington: GPO, 2008), p. 8.

[54] "Public Bills and Resolutions," Congressional Record, vol. 116, part. 12 (May 19, 1970), p. 16193.

[55] U.S. Congress, House, Committee on Rules, Amending Clause 19 of Rule XI of the Rules of the House of Representatives with Respect of Lobbying Practices and Political Campaign Contributions Affecting the House of Representatives and for Other Purposes, report to accompany H.Res. 1031, 91st Cong., 2nd sess., June 11, 1970, H.Rept. 91-1186 (Washington: GPO, 1970).

[56] "Lobbying Practices and Political Campaign Contributions Affecting the House of Representatives," Congressional Record, vol. 116, part 17 (July 8, 1970), pp. 23136-23141.

[57] "Rules of the House," Congressional Record, vol. 121, part 1 (January 14, 1975), p. 20.

[58] "Establishing a Select Committee on Ethics," Congressional Record, vol. 123, part 6, (March 9, 1977), pp. 6811- 6817.

[59] "Rules of the House," Congressional Record, vol. 123, January 4, 1977, p. 53. The committee continued to retain substantive jurisdiction over financial disclosure pursuant to the Ethics in Government Act of 1978 (P.L. 95-521, 92 Stat. 1824, October 26, 1978).

[60] "Providing for Consideration of House Resolution 287, to Amend the Rules of the House of Representatives," Congressional Record, vol. 123, part 5 (March 2, 1977), pp. 5885-5953.

[61] The Clerk of the House maintains the public repository for House financial disclosure reports pursuant to 5 U.S.C. app. §101 et seq. For more information on financial disclosure statements, see U.S. Congress, Clerk of the House of Representatives, "Financial Disclosure Reports," http://clerk.house.gov/public_disc/financial.html.

[62] H.Res. 383 (95th Congress). U.S. Congress, House Committee on Rules, Establishing a Select Committee on Ethics, report to accompany H.Res. 383, 95th Cong., 1st sess., March 8, 1977, H.Rept. 95-61 (Washington: GPO, 1977); and "Establishing a Select Committee on Ethics," Congressional Record, vol. 123, part 6 (March 9, 1977), pp. 6811-6817.

[63] "Amending the Rules of the House of Representatives and Establish a Permanent a Permanent Select Committee on Intelligence, Congressional Record, vol. 123, part 18 (July 14, 1977), pp. 22932-22949.

[64] Ibid., p. 22934.

[65] P.L. 95-105, 91 Stat. 863, August 17, 1977.

[66] P.L. 95-105, 91 Stat. 864, August 17, 1977.

[67] P.L. 95-521, 92 Stat. 1824, October 26, 1978; 5 U.S.C. app. §101.

[68] "Rules of the House," Congressional Record, vol. 125, part 1 (January 15, 1979), p. 9.

[69] P.L. 112-105, 126 Stat. 291, April 4, 2012. The STOCK Act has been amended three times to change the effective date for financial disclosure forms required under the act. First, P.L. 112-173 (126 Stat. 1310, August 16, 2012) extended the filing date to September 30, 2012. Second, P.L. 112-178 (126 Stat. 1408, September 28, 2012) extended the required filing

date to December 8, 2012. Finally, P.L. 112-207 (126 Stat. 1495, December 7, 2012) extended the required filing date to April 15, 2013. For a more detailed analysis of the STOCK Act, see CRS Report R42495, The STOCK Act, Insider Trading, and Public Financial Reporting by Federal Officials, by Jack Maskell.

[70] P.L. 112-105, Section 3; 5 U.S.C. app. 101 note prec.

[71] U.S. Congress, House Committee on Ethics, Periodic Reporting of Personal Financial Transactions Pursuant to the STOCK Act, as amended, 112th Cong., 2nd sess. (August 17, 2012), at http://ethics.house.gov/sites/ethics.house.gov/ files/PTR%20amended%20pink%20sheet.pdf

[72] P.L. 101-194, 103 Stat. 1716, November 30, 1989. The Ethics Reform Act, also mandated certain changes in the committee's procedures, infra. See U.S. Congress, House, Report of the Bipartisan Task Force on Ethics on H.R. 3360, committee print, 101st Cong., 1st sess. (Washington: GPO, 1989), pp. 9-11, 16-21; and "Government Ethics Reform Act of 1989," Congressional Record, vol. 135, part 21 (November 16, 1989), pp. 29469-29509.

[73] U.S. Congress, House Bipartisan Task Force on Ethics, H.R. 3660, to Amend the Rules of the House of Representatives and the Ethics in Government Act of 1978 to Provide for Government-Wide Ethics Reform, and for Other Purposes, committee print, 101st Cong., 1st sess., November 15, 1989 (Washington: GPO, 1989), pp. 4-5.

[74] U.S. Congress, House, Constitution, Jefferson's Manual, and Rules of the House of Representatives One Hundred Eleventh Congress, prepared by John V. Sullivan, Parliamentarian, 110th Cong., 2nd sess., H.Doc. 110-162 (Washington: GPO, 2009), §806, pp. 567-596; and U.S. Congress, House Committee on Standards of Official Conduct, Rules, 111th Cong., 1st sess., June 9, 2009 (http://ethics.house.gov/Media/PDF/ 111th_Rules_Amended_June_2009.pdf).

[75] U.S. Congress, House, Select Committee on Committees, Committee Reform Amendments of 1974, report to accompany H.Res. 988, 93rd Cong., 2nd sess., March 19, 1974, H.Rept. 93-916, Part 1 (Washington: GPO, 1974); U.S. Congress, House Select Committee on Committees, Committee Reform Amendments of 1974, report to accompany H.Res. 988, 93rd Cong., 2nd sess., March 19, 1974, H.Rept. 93-916, Part 2 (Washington: GPO, 1974); and "Committee Reform Amendments of 1974," Congressional Record, vol. 120, part 26 (October 8, 1974), pp. 34447-34470.

[76] U.S. Congress, House, Select Committee on Committees, Committee Reform Amendments of 1974, report to accompany H.Res. 988, 93rd Cong., 2nd sess., March 19, 1974, H.Rept. 93-916, Part 2 (Washington: GPO, 1974), p. 176. See also "Committee Reform Amendments of 1974," Congressional Record, vol. 120, part 26 (October 8, 1974), pp. 34406-34420; and "Committee Reform Amendments of 1974," Congressional Record, vol. 120, part 26 (October 8, 1974), pp. 34447-34470. Previously, an affirmative vote of 10 Members of the 12 Member panel were required for approving committee reports, issuing recommendations or advisory opinions, and initiating investigations. See footnote 47 for more information.

[77] "Rules of the House," Congressional Record, vol. 123, part 1 (January 4, 1977), p. 53.

[78] "Rules of the House," Congressional Record, vol. 125, part 1 (January 15, 1979), p. 8.

[79] P.L. 101-194, 103 Stat. 1716, November 30, 1989. For the debate on the Ethics Reform Act of 1989, see "Government Ethics Reform Act of 1989," House debate, Congressional Record, vol. 135, part 21, (November 16, 1989), pp. 29468-29513; "Government Ethics Reform Act of 1989," Senate debate, Congressional Record, vol. 135, part 21, (November 17, 1989), pp. 29660-29678; and 29681-29707; and "Government Ethics Reform Act," Senate debate, Congressional Record, vol. 135, part 21 (November 17, 1979), pp. 29777-29796.

[80] P.L. 101-194, Section 803(i), 103 Stat. 1775, November 30, 1989; 2 U.S.C. §29d.

[81] For more information on the Office of Advice and Education, see U.S. Congress, House, Committee on Ethics, "About: Committee Advice," 111th Cong., 2nd sess. (http://ethics.house.gov/About/Default.aspx?Section=8); and U.S. Congress, House, Committee on Standards of Official Conduct, Summary of Activities, One Hundred Tenth Congress, 110th Cong., 2nd sess., January 3, 2009, H.Rept. 110-938 (Washington: GPO, 2009).

[82] Bifurcation is the separation of administrative and investigative functions of the Committee on Ethics. The Ethics Task Force defined bifurcation as: "... a 'firewall' between the Committee functions of investigation and adjudication, ensuring that Committee members who charge a respondent with a violation do not also participate in a judgment of whether liability has been established. It also allocates responsibility within the Committee so that the review of information offered as a complaint is less time-consuming for members of the Committee and is consistent with the confidentiality imposed on the complaint process. For these reasons, the Task Force encourages Committee members to protect the integrity of the 'firewall' to the greatest degree possible." See U.S. Congress, House, Committee on Rules, Report of the Ethics Reform Task Force on H.Res. 168, committee print, 105th Cong., 1st sess., June 17, 1997 (Washington: GPO, 1997), p. 7.

[83] P.L. 101-194, Section 803(e), 103 Stat. 1774, November 30, 1989.

[84] P.L. 101-194, Section 803(g), 103 Stat. 1775, November 30, 1989.

[85] Ibid. For information on "Letters of Reproval," see CRS Report RL30764, Enforcement of Congressional Rules of Conduct: An Historical Overview, by Jacob R. Straus.

[86] P.L. 101-194, Section 803(a), 103 Stat. 1773, November 30, 1989. House Rule X, clause 5. Democratic Caucus Rules include additional limits on committee service.

[87] P.L. 101-194, 103 Stat. 1774, November 30, 1989; 2 U.S.C. §29d.

[88] "Imp lementing the Recommendations of Bipartisan House Ethics Task Force," Congressional Record, vol. 143, September 18, 1997, pp. 19302-19340.

[89] Rep. Richard Armey, "Creation of Bipartisan Task Force to Review Ethics Process," Congressional Record, vol. 143, part 2 (February 12, 1997), p. 2059.

[90] "Creation of Bipartisan Task Force to Review Ethics Process," Congressional Record, vol. 143, part 2 (February 12, 1997), pp. 2058-2059.

[91] Rep. Richard Armey, "Creation of Bipartisan Task Force to Review Ethics Process," Congressional Record, vol. 143, part 2 (February 12, 1997), p. 2059.

[92] U.S. Congress, House Ethics Reform Task Force on H.Res. 168, Recommending Revisions to the Rules of the House and the Rules of the Committee on Standards of Official Conduct with Additional Views, committee print, 105th Cong., 1st sess., June 17, 1997 (Washington: GPO, 1997), pp. 4-5.

[93] "Providing for Consideration of H.Res. 168, Implementing the Recommendations of Bipartisan House Ethics Reform Task Force," Congressional Record, vol. 143, part 13 (September 18, 1997), pp. 19302-19310.

[94] "Implementing the Recommendations of Bipartisan House Ethics Task Force," Congressional Record, vol. 143, part 13 (September 18, 1997), pp. 19310-19340.

[95] H.Res. 168, Section 9 (105th Congress), agreed to September 17, 1997. This procedure superseded a process whereby non-House Members could file complaints with the Committee on Standards only after submitting allegations to at least three House Members, who had refused in writing to transmit the complaint to the committee.

[96] "Rules of the House," Congressional Record, vol. 145, part 1 (January 6, 1999), p. 54. The formal change in membership from 12 to 10 codified the defacto size of the committee in the 105th Congress even though the Ethics Reform Act of 1989 required each party to

nominate seven Members for the committee (P.L. 101-194, Section 803(b), 103 Stat. 1774, November 30, 1989; 2 U.S.C. §29d).

[97] H.Res. 168, Section 1(a) (105th Congress), agreed to September 17, 1997. The first pool of 20 Members selected to serve on investigative committees of the Standards Committee was appointed on November 13, 1997. For a list of initial appointments, see Speaker Pro Tempore [Rep. Ray La Hood], "List of Republican and Democratic Members Selected to Serve As 'Pool' For Purposes Relating To The Committee on Standards of Official Conduct," Congressional Record, vol. 143, November 13, 1997, p. 26569. The House leadership has subsequently appointed a 20- person pool of Members in each Congress.

[98] H.Res. 168, Section 10 (105th Congress), agreed to September 17, 1997. Previously, there was no specific time limit for this determination.

[99] H.Res. 168, Section 18 (105th Congress), agreed to September 17, 1997. With the exception of a brief period in 1966, only a vote by the full House previously permitted referrals of possible violations of law to the appropriate authorities.

[100] H.Res. 168, Section 4 (105th Congress), agreed to September 17, 1997.

[101] H.Res. 168, Section 3 and Section 11 (105th Congress), agreed to September 17, 1997.

[102] H.Res. 168, Section 2 (105th Congress), agreed to September 17, 1997. When the House adopted its rules for the 106th Congress (1999-2001), it changed the committee service rule and also voted to eliminate the rule requiring four members of the Standards Committee to rotate off the committee every Congress. This action returned the committee's service requirement to what it had been after the adoption of the Ethics Reform Act of 1989 (no more than three Congresses in any period of five successive Congresses). See "Rules of the House," Congressional Record, vol. 145, part 1 (January 6, 1999), p. 54. House Democratic Caucus Rules further limit service on the Committee on Standards.

[103] "Rules of the House," Congressional Record, daily edition, vol. 151(January 4, 2005), pp. H8-H10.

[104] H.Res. 240 (109th Congress), agreed to April 27, 2005 with the adoption of H.Res. 241. "Amending the Rules of the House of Representatives to Reinstate Certain Provision of the Rules Relating to Procedures of the Committee on Standards of Official Conduct to the Form in which those Provisions Existed at the Close of the 108th Congress," Congressional Record, daily edition, vol. 151 (April 27, 2005), pp. H2616-H2626.

[105] H.Res. 451 (110th Congress), agreed to June 5, 2007.

[106] H.Res. 5 (111th Congress), agreed to January 6, 2009; "Rules of the House," Congressional Record, vol. 155 (January 6, 2009), p. H6-H10. H.Res. 5 (112th Congress), agreed to January 5, 2011; "Rules of the House," Congressional Record, daily edition, vol. 157 (January 5, 2011), p. H7.

[107] H.Res. 5, Section 2(e)(2), (113th Congress), agreed to on January 3, 2013; "Rules of the House," Congressional Record, daily edition, vol. 159 (January 3, 2013), p. H6.

[108] H.Res. 5, Section 2(e)(3), (113th Congress), agreed to January 3, 2013.

[109] U.S. Congress, Speaker of the House of Representatives, "Pelosi Announces Special Task Force on Ethics Enforcement," press release, January 31, 2007, http://speaker.house.gov/newsroom/pressreleases?id=0057.

[110] The other Members of the task force were Representatives Bobby Scott, Marty Meehan, Betty McCollum, Lamar Smith (ranking member), Dave Camp, Dave Hobson, and Todd Tiahrt. Representative David Price was appointed to the task force in July 2007, when Representative Meehan resigned from Congress.

[111] U.S. Congress, House Special Task Force on Ethics Enforcement, Report of the Democratic Members of the Special Task Force on Ethics Enforcement, committee print, 110th Cong.,

1st sess., H.Prt. 110-1 (Washington: GPO, 2007), pp. 4-5. Subsequently, on February 27, 2008, ranking member Rep. Lamar Smith and the other Republican Members of the task force introduced H.Res. 1003, to provide increased accountability and transparency in the Committee on Standards of Official Conduct. On March 3, 2008, Representative Capuano also released proposed amendments to H.Res. 895. For more information on the proposed amendments, see Rep. Michael E. Capuano, "Amendments to the Proposed Reforms to the Ethics Process," Dear Colleague letter, March 3, 2008, http://www.house.gov/ capuano/ news/2008/ pr121907-letter030308.pdf.

[112] "Establishing an Office of Congressional Ethics," Congressional Record, daily edition, vol. 154 (March 11, 2008), pp. H1515-H1536.

[113] U.S. Congress, Speaker of the House of Representatives, "Pelosi, Boehner Announce Appointments to New Office of Congressional Ethics," press release, July 24, 2008, http://speaker.house.gov/newsroom/pressreleases?id=0762. The members are former Representatives David Skaggs (chair), Porter Goss (vice chair), Karan English, and Yvonne Brathwaite Burke; former House Chief Administrative Officer Jay Eagen; and former professor and chief of staff of the Federal Election Commission Allison Hayward. The alternates are former Representative and federal judge Abner Mikva and former Representative Bill Frenzel. Board members are appointed at the beginning of each Congress.

[114] H.Res. 5, Section 4(d), (113th Congress), agreed to January 3, 2013; "Rules of the House" Congressional Record, daily edition, vol. 159 (January 3, 2013), p. H6. For more information on the Office of Congressional Ethics, see CRS Report R40760, House Office of Congressional Ethics: History, Authority, and Procedures, by Jacob R. Straus.

[115] Because all Members must be reappointed to the committee in subsequent Congress, this total counts Members who served in more than one Congress multiple times. The number of Members on the committee has fluctuated over time as the result of Members leaving the committee or being temporarily replaced due to conflict of interest for cases before the committee.

In: U.S. House of Representatives
Editor: Bruno Montagne

ISBN: 978-1-62808-364-4

Chapter 2

HOUSE OFFICE OF CONGRESSIONAL ETHICS: HISTORY, AUTHORITY, AND PROCEDURES*

Jacob R. Straus

SUMMARY

The House Office of Congressional Ethics (OCE) was established on March 11, 2008, with the passage of H.Res. 895. It was reauthorized by the House as part of the rules package (H.Res. 5) adopted by the 113th Congress on January 3, 2013.

This action followed years of efforts by groups within and outside Congress to create an independent entity to investigate allegations of misconduct by members, officers, and employees of Congress. During the 110th Congress (2007-2008), Speaker of the House Nancy Pelosi and Minority Leader John Boehner created the bipartisan Special Task Force on Ethics Enforcement, chaired by Representative Michael Capuano, to consider whether the House should create an "outside" ethics-enforcement entity. The task force worked for nearly a year before issuing its recommendations for the creation of the OCE.

The mandate of the OCE, which has jurisdiction only in the House, is to review information, and when appropriate, refer findings of fact to the

---

* This is an edited, reformatted and augmented version of a Congressional Research Service publication, CRS Report for Congress R40760, prepared for Members and Committees of Congress, from www.crs.gov, dated March 8, 2013.

House Committee on Ethics. Only this committee, pursuant to House rules, has the authority to recommend House discipline of members and staff. Information of alleged wrongdoing by members, officers, and employees of the House may be accepted by the OCE from the general public, but only the OCE board can initiate a review.

The OCE is composed of six board members, and at least two alternates, each of whom serves a four-year term. The Speaker and the minority leader are each responsible for the appointment of three board members and one alternate. The chair is selected by the Speaker and a co-chair is selected by the minority leader. Current members of the House, federal employees, and lobbyists are not eligible to serve on the board.

OCE rules for the conduct of investigations and code of conduct can be found at their website, http://oce.house.gov.

This report describes the history and rationale behind the creation of the OCE, its operations, and its relationship with the House Committee on Ethics, and options potentially available for Congress if further amendments to the House ethics process are desired.

INTRODUCTION

In the *Federalist Papers*, James Madison commented that "no man is allowed to be a judge in his own case, because his interest would certainly bias his judgment, and, not improbably, corrupt his integrity. With equal, nay with greater reason, a body of men are unfit to be both judge and parties at the same time."[1] Since the first session of Congress in 1789, the House of Representatives and the Senate have contemplated how to judge fellow members. Appropriately, investigating and judging members of Congress continues to be an issue for Congress.

In 1964, the Senate established the Select Committee on Ethics,[2] and in 1967, the House created the Committee on Standards of Official Conduct,[3] which was renamed the Committee on Ethics in the 112th Congress (2011-2012).[4] These two committees formally assumed the duties of investigating allegations of wrongdoing against members of their respective chambers. In the House, the Committee on Ethics has had sole responsibility to investigate and recommend the discipline of members.[5] Self-discipline by the Committee on Ethics has, at various times, been considered problematic, as members are dependent on one another to do their jobs, bring individual perspectives on chamber rules to investigations, and are judged by the public at the same time they are judging congressional colleagues.[6] This creates a difficult investigative environment and often leads to closed-door investigations and media allegations of improper enforcement of chamber rules.[7] Historically, Congress has used its ethics power neither arbitrarily nor frequently. Congress has, however, "periodically tightened its ethics codes and procedures for dealing with misconduct."[8]

In addition to amending internal congressional ethics codes and procedures, Congress has considered numerous legislative proposals since 1951 to create an independent ethics advisory body that would replace or assist the Committee on Ethics with investigations or enforcement.

In the 110th Congress (2007-2008), the House created the Office of Congressional Ethics (OCE) to review complaints, and when appropriate, refer findings of fact to the Committee on Ethics. The OCE is the first independent, outside body charged by Congress to investigate complaints against members and refer valid complaints to the Committee on Ethics.

The OCE is intended to perform an important public service for the House and the public by assuring the integrity of the chamber.[9] It provides a way for groups and individuals to provide information about alleged misconduct by members, officers, and employees of the House to an investigative body. The office is designed to "supplement but not supplant" the role of the House Committee on Ethics.[10] The OCE formally opened on January 23, 2009, after adopting rules for conducting investigations and a code of conduct for its board members and staff.[11] It has jurisdiction only over current members, officers, and employees of the House. This report focuses only on the House of Representatives and the House ethics process.

Previous Legislative Attempts for Outside or Independent Enforcement of Congressional Rules of Conduct

Since the establishment of the Senate Select Committee on Ethics and the House Committee on Ethics, members of both committees have sometimes been perceived as reluctant to investigate and discipline colleagues.[12] Seeking to be fair and not to pre-judge or prejudice the consideration of an allegation, the committees operate with little publicity. As a result they have often been criticized by the media for "failure to properly implement and enforce the internal rules of their respective house of Congress."[13] Until 2008, these perceptions led to unsuccessful calls for investigative and enforcement mechanisms to supplement or replace the ethics committees.

Over the years, proposals have been offered to create an office of public integrity, an independent ethics commission, and a public review board or office within the legislative branch, composed of former Members of Congress, retired judges, private citizens, or a combination of these.[14] For some, having a panel of senior statesmen help investigate allegations of wrongdoing by Members of Congress is viewed as a way to strengthen Congress.[15] Dennis Thompson, a Harvard professor of public policy and congressional scholar, has long advocated countering the institutional conflict of interest inherent in Members judging Members with an independent body such as an ethics commission. Thompson sees such an outside body as

> likely to reach more objective and independent judgments. It could more credibly protect members' rights and enforce institutional obligations without regard to political or personal loyalties. It would provide more effective accountability and help restore the confidence of the public. And—an advantage that should appeal to Congress—it would reduce the time members would have to spend on the chores of ethics regulation.[16]

Beginning in 1951, even before the ethics committees were created, there were legislative proposals to create an independent entity to investigate complaints in both the House and the Senate or within one house. None of these were enacted. Only the legislative proposals that prompted hearings are discussed below. Proposals receiving no committee action are listed in *Table 1* and *Table 2.*

Congress-Wide Proposals

Between 1951 and 1996, several proposals were introduced in both the House and Senate to create a bicameral independent ethics panel. In 1951, Senate hearings were held on a proposal to create a Commission on Ethics in Government. In 1993, 42 years later, the Joint Committee on the Organization of Congress held hearings on the congressional ethics process. *Table 1* also lists legislation introduced to create a Congress-wide independent ethics entity.

Commission on Ethics in Government

In the 82nd Congress (1951-1952), Senator J. William Fulbright introduced S.Con.Res. 21, to create a congressional commission to "strengthen the faith and confidence of the American people in their Government by assisting in the establishment of higher moral standards in the official conduct of the executive and legislative branches of the Government."[17] The resolution was referred to the Senate Committee on Labor and Human Resources, where a special subcommittee was established to examine the resolution. Chaired by Senator Paul Douglas, the Special Subcommittee on the Establishment of a Commission on Ethics in Government held a series of hearings in June and July of 1951. In his introductory remarks, Senator Douglas summarized the importance of ethical standards and why the hearings would focus on more than just Senator Fulbright's concurrent resolution.

> I think the time has come for positive proposals to deal with the ethical problems of government. This should include not merely the executive agencies, but the Congress itself—because if we investigate others, we should be willing to submit ourselves to investigation—and all private citizens. We all have a great stake in lifting the standards of our governmental performance.[18]

Following the hearings, the subcommittee endorsed the passage of S.Con.Res. 21 and the creation of a commission on ethics in government. The subcommittee recommended that

> A Commission on Ethics in Government should be established by joint resolution of Congress. The Commission's function should be twofold, the first to investigate and report to the President and to the Congress on the moral standards of official conduct of officers and employees of the United States; the effect thereon of the moral standards in business and political activity of persons and groups doing business with the Government or seeking to influence public policy and administration; and the moral standards generally prevailing in society which condition the conduct of public affairs or which affect the strength and unity of the Nation.
>
> ... The second function of the Commission should be to recommend measures to improve and maintain at a high level moral standards of official conduct in the Federal Government and of all persons who participate in or are responsible for the conduct of public affairs. It should be noted that the Commission would not be concerned with the morals of individuals—governmental personnel or private citizens—except as they are involved in the conduct of public affairs.[19]

In addition to recommending the creation of a commission, the subcommittee also recommended amendments to the Administrative Procedure Act;[20] mandatory disclosure of income, assets, and certain transactions by members of Congress and certain federal officials; a thorough study of proposed changes to criminal law governing conflict of interest and bribery laws; creation of a citizens' organization to work for better government on the national level; and 12 measures related to ethics issues that merited additional study and consideration.[21] S.Con.Res. 21 was not debated further in either the full committee or on the Senate floor.

Joint Committee on the Organization of Congress

In 1993, the Joint Committee on the Organization of Congress held hearings on the congressional ethics process[22] that included former and incumbent Members of Congress, as well as academic scholars. Their testimonies dealt with the advantages and disadvantages of independent ethics entities and how an outside body might assist the ethics committees in the enforcement of congressional rules of conduct. The joint committee's final report summarized the differing opinions of witnesses on the role of an independent entity and its ramifications on Congress:

> While no witnesses advocated giving the entire responsibility to a group of outsiders, some wanted non-members to be able to investigate charges and recommend punishment. Representative Robert Andrews, when testifying in favor of an external ethics commission, said, "Our system purports to conduct review of ethics by our peers, but I think we misdefine what it means to be a peer. Ultimately, our peers are not fellow Representatives or Senators, ultimately our peers are ordinary citizens." Conversely, other witnesses wanted ethics proceedings to be conducted only by members. As former Senator Warren Rudman testified,
>
> "I believe that the Constitution, when it says that we ought to be the judge of our own members, means precisely what it says." A former Chairman of the Standards of Official Conduct Committee, Representative Louis Stokes was "troubled by calls for further procedural reforms, which are based on the notion that the Ethics Committee has not done its job or has not done it properly."[23]

Subsequently, the House members of the committee recommended that "the Committee on Standards of Official Conduct should be authorized to use, on a discretionary basis, a panel of non-members in ethics cases."[24] No further action was taken on any of the ethics proposals discussed by the joint committee.[25]

Table 1. Selected Legislative Proposals for a Congress-Wide Independent Ethics Entity

Congress	Bill Number	Date Introduced	Sponsor
96th (1979-1980)	S.J.Res. 144	February 6, 1980	William Roth (R-DE)
109th (2005-2006)	S.Con.Res. 82	February 28, 2006	John Kerry (D-MA)
	H.R. 4799	February 16, 2006	Christopher Shays (R-CT)
	H.R. 5677	June 22, 2006	Christopher Shays (R-CT)
	S. 2259	February 8, 2006	Barack Obama (D-IL)

Source: Library of Congress, (LIS) Legislative Information System of the U.S. Congress, http://www.congress.gov.

Table 2. Selected Legislative Proposals for a House Independent Ethics Entity

Congress	Bill Number	Date Introduced	Sponsor
100th (1987-1988)	H.Res. 526	August 11, 1988	Joseph DioGuardi (R-NY)
102nd (1991-1992)	H.Res. 465	May 21, 1992	Curt Weldon (R-PA)
103rd (1993-1994)	H.Res. 43	January 25, 1993	Curt Weldon (R-PA)
104th (1995-1996)	H.Res. 95	February 23, 1995	Curt Weldon (R-PA)
	H.R. 2797	December 15, 1995	Harold Volkmer (D-MO)
105th (1997-1998)	H.Res. 41	February 5, 1997	Curt Weldon (R-PA)
	H.Res. 61	February 13, 1997	Lee Hamilton (D-IN)
	H.R. 957	March 5, 1997	Christopher Shays (R-CT)
109th (2005-2006)	H.R. 2412	May 17, 2005	Marty Meehan (D-MA)
	H.R. 4920	March 9, 2006	Michael Castle (R-DE)
	H.R. 4948	March 14, 2006	Earl Blumenauer (D-OR)
110th (2007-2008)	H.Res. 895	December 19, 2007	Michael Capuano (D-MA)
	H.Res. 1018	March 4, 2008	Baron Hill (D-IN)
	H.R. 97	January 1, 2007	Michael Castle (R-DE)
	H.R. 1136	February 16, 2007	Earl Blumenauer (D-OR)
	H.R. 1754	March 29, 2007	Baron Hill (D-IN)
	H.R. 2544	May 24, 2007	Joe Sestak (D-PA)
	H.R. 2822	June 21, 2007	Joe Sestak (D-PA)
	H.R. 4239	November 15, 2007	Christopher Murphy (D-CT)

Source: Library of Congress, (LIS) Legislative Information System of the U.S. Congress, http://www.congress.gov.

House Proposals

Prior to the passage of H.Res. 895 in the 110th Congress (2007-2008), the House considered numerous proposals to create an independent ethics commission. These proposals ranged in scope and included proposals to abolish the Committee on Standards of Official Conduct, authorize an independent entity for all ethics issues, and create an independent entity to work with the committee. Prior to H.Res. 895, none of the proposals received further consideration after being referred to committee. *Table 2* lists proposals that were offered between 1988 and 2007 to create an independent ethics entity in the House.

While none of the legislative proposals listed in *Table 2* moved beyond introduction, in 2007, the Speaker of the House and the minority leader restarted the conversation about an independent ethics entity by creating a Special Task Force on Ethics Enforcement. The result of the task force's work was the introduction of H.Res. 895 (110th Congress) and the creation of the Office of Congressional Ethics (OCE) to collect information from the public; investigate Members, officers, and staff of the House of Representatives; and provide that information to the House Committee on Ethics.

SPECIAL TASK FORCE ON ETHICS ENFORCEMENT

On January 31, 2007, House Speaker Nancy Pelosi and Minority Leader John Boehner announced the creation of the Special Task Force on Ethics Enforcement in the House of Representatives. Chaired by Representative Michael Capuano, the task force was charged with considering "whether the House should create an outside enforcement entity, based on examples in state legislatures and private entities."[26]

During the next eight months, the task force met 29 times in executive session to discuss the investigative process and to hear from current and former Members of Congress, academic experts, and citizen advocacy groups.[27] The executive sessions both preceded and followed a public hearing in April 2007.

Establishment of the task force was part of Speaker Nancy Pelosi's emphasis on ethics reform in the 110th Congress and followed several congressional scandals in the previous Congresses.[28] In January 2006, congressional Democrats from around the country joined in a Washington, DC press conference to pledge "honest leadership and open government."[29] At the same time, Public Citizen, the watchdog group, issued a list of six benchmarks for reform which included the establishment of an independent congressional Office of Public Integrity to monitor allegations of ethics violations and refer them to the congressional ethics committees.[30] Public opinion also appeared to favor reform, as a January 2006 *CNN/USAToday/Gallup* poll found that "corruption in government" was ranked as an "extremely important" or "very important" issue by 81% of respondents.[31]

Hearing

On April 19, 2007, the Special Task Force on Ethics Enforcement held a public hearing to discuss "whether the House should create an independent entity relative to the ethics process, and if so, what form, makeup, authority, et cetera, that entity should be."[32] In his opening remarks, Ranking Member Lamar Smith summarized both the positive and negative aspects of creating an independent ethics entity in the House.

> Today we examine proposals to create an independent ethics commission. I know there are some independent legislative ethics commissions operating ... that would have been considered a success. But I also know there are unique items at work in Washington, DC, and issues of Federal law that do not apply elsewhere. I know some see the need for a commission that operates independently of the duly elected membership of the House of Representatives. Yet I also know there are those who are concerned that the ethics enforcement entity not be so independent from duly elected members that it upsets the checks and balances. That system must exist within our Constitution which requires separation of powers among the executive, judicial and legislative branches.[33]

The task force heard from four witnesses, three in favor of an independent ethics entity and one who was opposed. Testifying in favor of an independent entity were Tom Fitton, president of Judicial Watch; Meredith McGehee, policy director of the Campaign Legal Center; and Fred Wertheimer, president of Democracy 21. They each spoke of their belief that creating an independent, impartial, and investigative entity would end the conflict of interest that exists when members are asked to judge their colleagues. For example, Tom Fitton testified that the "House ethics process is broken and in need of reform," and that "[a]s this Task Force considers ways for the House to honor its constitutional obligation to uphold its own rules of conduct, I respectfully suggest you strongly consider an independent entity, answerable to House members, which can undertake investigations and make independent findings and recommendations for action to the appropriate House body."[34]

Testifying against an independent ethics entity was Don Wolfensberger, director of the Congress Project at the Woodrow Wilson International Center for Scholars. Mr. Wolfensberger stated,

> The bottom line is that the power of Congress to punish its members is rooted in the need to protect the institution from actions and behavior that would bring the body into disrepute or disarray. It is not a power that can be properly exercised, even in part, by non-members for the very reason that only members have the institutional sense, instincts, and legitimacy to exercise it correctly and effectively for the good of the House. Others would tend to confine themselves to the question of justice for the individual member accused.[35]

Mr. Wolfensberger further suggested that the House ethics process could be strengthened if

- the chair and ranking member kept the full committee membership apprised of the status of all complaints filed with the committee;
- the full committee determined when an investigative subcommittee should be created;
- an investigative subcommittee was not allowed to enter into an agreement with a respondent, but instead recommended a proposed settlement that the full committee could finalize, modify, or reject;
- when an investigative subcommittee report did not adopt a statement of alleged violation, it should be sent to the House (and public) and not to the full committee; and
- the committee's authority to issue a letter of reproval or other appropriate action be available, as a matter of privilege, for possible House action.[36]

Following the hearing, Representative Capuano received a letter signed by 27 House Democrats asking the task force to "address the structural flaws that underlie the current enforcement process."

Our current ethics process is also out of step with how these matters are handled in almost half the state legislatures. The experience in the states has proven that effective safeguards can be put in place to deter potential abuse of the ethics process without undermining its integrity and free of any constitutional concerns. Under such a revamped ethics process, final determination of any alleged ethical misconduct would remain the responsibility of the members, as is constitutionally required. We believe that building greater independence into the ethics enforcement process, especially in the investigatory phase, is an appropriate response to the problems of the past and will be a safeguard against any recurrences.[37]

Final Report

In December 2007, the Special Task Force on Ethics Enforcement issued its final report. Only the Democratic members of the task force, however, penned their names to the report. The Republican members chose to withhold comment.[38] The report recommended the creation of an Office of Congressional Ethics (OCE) as an independent office within the House to "review information on allegations of misconduct by members, officers, and employees of the House and make recommendations to the Committee on Standards of Official Conduct for the Committee's official consideration and action."[39]

The task force proposed a six-member entity to investigate possible violations of House rules. The report stated that "[t]he new Office of Congressional Ethics will act as an origination point for independent review of possible violations of standards of conduct, but will not prevent the Standards Committee from accepting complaints filed by members."[40] In a press release accompanying the report, Representative Capuano reported that the task force was recommending that

- a nonpartisan professional staff be hired by the panel, and current House members and lobbyists not be permitted to serve on the panel;
- the OCE conduct preliminary reviews, then refer all matters subject to a second-phase review to the Committee on Standards for disposition; if no merit is found, the board may recommend dismissal;
- the OCE be given up to 30 calendar days or 5 legislative days, whichever was greater, to conduct a preliminary review, and 45

calendar days or 5 legislative days to review a matter in the second phase before referral to the Committee on Standards;

- the Committee on Standards be given up to 45 calendar or 5 legislative days, whichever was greater, to consider the matter as allowed pursuant to current Committee on Standards Rules 16b-16e; and
- the Committee on Standards be required to make a public statement, or finding, on referrals from the OCE by the end of the 45-calendar-day or 5-legislative-day period.[41]

H.Res. 895

In coordination with the release of the task force members' report recommending the creation of an independent ethics entity, Representative Capuano introduced H.Res. 895 on December 19, 2007. In preparation for a Committee on Rules hearing on H.Res. 895, Representative Capuano sent a Dear Colleague letter[42] in March 2008 and wrote an opinion article in *Roll Call*[43] advocating adoption of the task force's recommendations for an independent ethics entity. On March 10, the Committee on Rules reported H.Res. 1031, which provided for adoption of H.Res. 895, as amended, with a recommendation that the resolution be adopted.[44]

The Committee on Rules report included amendments to H.Res. 895 that were to be considered as adopted. The amendments made 13 changes to the original text of H.Res. 895. A comparison of the amendments adopted by the Committee on Rules and the original language, as proposed by Representative Capuano, can be found in the *Appendix*.

On March 11, 2008, the House debated and agreed to H.Res. 1031, which provided for the adoption of H.Res. 895, as amended under a closed, self-executing rule.[45] In his remarks following the passage of H.Res. 895, Representative Capuano stated,

> Tonight's passage of H.Res. 895 establishing an Office of Congressional Ethics (OCE) represents the most dramatic progress in years in the drive to strengthen ethics enforcement in the House. It is the culmination of many months of deliberation and review by the Special Task Force on Ethics Enforcement, created jointly by Speaker Pelosi and Minority Leader Boehner. I strongly believe that the approach we have taken to ethics enforcement will improve the reputation of the House and

will break the appearance of an 'old boy network' forever. The OCE brings a level of independence to the process because no current members of Congress can serve on the panel. It also brings a level of transparency that is sorely lacking in the current process by requiring that a public statement be issued on most matters reviewed by the OCE. Taken together, these two fundamental elements will go a long way toward restoring the public's confidence in the people's House.[46]

Office of Congressional Ethics

The OCE held its first public meeting on January 23, 2009, and began to implement the structural requirements of H.Res. 895. It also adopted rules of procedure, a code of conduct, and rules for the conduct of a review. The Office of Congressional Ethics (OCE) was reauthorized by the House as part of the rules package (H.Res. 5) adopted by the 113th Congress on January 3, 2013.[47] The following sections outline the structure, powers, authority, and procedures of the OCE.

Structure

The OCE is structured to be nonpartisan. This goal is reflected in the composition of the board's membership, leadership schema, statutory qualifications, employment status of its members and staff, and required oath (or affirmation) of office. In addition, the authorizing resolution specifies a particular hiring process and requires an oath (or affirmation) of staff that OCE information not be disclosed.

Board Membership

Six members and two alternates constitute the board. Each member may serve for four years, subject to reappointment at the beginning of each Congress.[48] Three members and an alternate are appointed by the Speaker, subject to the approval of the minority leader, and a like number are appointed by the minority leader, subject to the approval of the Speaker. Vacancies on the board are filled by the most senior alternate nominated by the same congressional leader who nominated the departing member. The alternate serves on the board until a replacement is named. If a permanent replacement is not named within 90 days of the vacancy, the alternate continues to serve for the remainder of the term, and the Speaker or minority leader, as applicable, will nominate a new alternate.[49] The Speaker and the minority leader, acting jointly, may remove a board member for cause.[50]

The OCE membership structure is designed to create an incentive for the Speaker and the minority leader to work together when choosing board members. Because no formal confirmation process was established in H.Res. 895, the nominations of the Speaker and the minority leader result in de facto appointments of chosen individuals to the board. Should the Speaker and the minority leader not concur on board appointments, potential exists for open positions, which could prevent the board from reaching a quorum.[51] *Table 3* lists the members of the board for the 113th Congress.

Table 3. Office of Congressional Ethics Board Membership 113th Congress (2013-2014)

Board Role	Name	Appointed by
Chair	Porter Goss	Speaker of the House
Co-Chair	David Skaggs	Minority Leader
	Yvonne Burke	Minority Leader
	Karen English	Minority Leader
	Jay Eagen	Speaker of the House
	Allison Hayward	Speaker of the House
Alternate	Mike Barnes	Minority Leader
Alternate	William Frenzel	Speaker of the House

Source: U.S. Congress, Speaker of the House of Representatives, “Boehner, Pelosi Announces Appointments to Office of Congressional Ethics,” press release, January 16, 2013, at http://www.speaker.gov/press-release/ boehner-pelosi-announces-appointments-office-congressional-ethics; and U.S. Congress, Office of the Minority Leader of the House of Reprsentatives, “Boehner, Pelosi Announce Appointments to Office of Congressional Ethics,” press release, January 16, 2013, at http://www.democraticleader.gov/ Boehner_Pelosi_ Announce_Appointments_to_OCE.

Pursuant to H.Res. 895 (110th Congress), Members of the OCE board are restricted to serving on the board for no more than four consecutive Congresses (two consecutive terms).[52] In the 113th Congress (2013-2014), with the adoption of H.Res. 5, the House waived the restriction that OCE board members may “not serve during more than four consecutive Congresses” and also allowed board members who were initially appointed in the 110th Congress—and therefore supposed to be ineligible to be appointed beyond the

112th Congress—to be reappointed through at least the 114th Congress (2015-2016).[53]

Oath of Office

Before board members begin their term, they are required to sign a document agreeing not to be a candidate for the U.S. Senate or the House of Representatives and execute an oath or affirmation on disclosure of information.

Copies of the signed document are retained by the Clerk of the House as part of the records of the House. The Clerk makes the documents available to the public, publishes the documents as part of the *Congressional Record*, and makes a cumulative list of names available on the Clerk's website.[54] The document contains the following statement:

> I agree not to be a candidate for the Office of Senator or Representative in, or Delegate or Resident Commissioner to, the Congress for purposes of the Federal Election Campaign Act of 1971 until at least 3 years after I am no longer a member of the board or staff of the Office of Congressional Ethics.[55]

Additionally, board members must execute an oath or affirmation in writing prior to assuming board responsibilities. Copies of the oath or affirmation are provided to the Clerk as part of the records of the House. The text of the oath is as follows:

> I do solemnly swear (or affirm) that I will not disclose to any person or entity outside of the Office any information received in the course of my service with the Office, except as authorized by the board as necessary to conduct official business or pursuant to its rules.[56]

Board Leadership

The board is led by a chair and a co-chair. The chair is designated by the Speaker and the co-chair is designated by the minority leader.[57] The chair, or a majority of board members, has the authority to call a board meeting.[58]

Qualifications

Board members are expected to be "individuals of exceptional public standing who are specifically qualified to serve on the board by virtue of their education, training, or experience in one or more of the following fields:

legislative, judicial, regulatory, professional ethics, business, legal, and academic."[59] Selection of board members is to be made without regard to political affiliation.[60]

Individuals are prohibited from serving as board members if they were (1) a registered lobbyist under the Lobbying Disclosure Act of 1995;[61] (2) registered as a lobbyist during the year prior to appointment; (3) engaged in lobbying, or employed to lobby Congress; (4) an agent of a foreign principal registered under the Foreign Agents Registration Act (FARA);[62] (5) a member of Congress; or (6) an officer or employee of the federal government.[63] Additionally, former members, officers, and employees of the House cannot be appointed to the board in the year following their time as a member, officer, or employee of the House.[64]

Restrictions on the political and outside activities of board members are designed to create the independent, nonpartisan group necessary to conduct investigations in an expeditious manner. As explained under "Investigative Procedure," the OCE has a short time frame to conduct investigations.

Employment Status

Members of the OCE board are not considered officers or employees of the House, but do receive remuneration for their service. Board members receive a per diem equal to the daily equivalent of the minimum rate of basic pay for GS-15 employees of the General Schedule for each day of service, including travel time. Pay is only for time when the board member is engaged in performance of duties for the board.[65]

Staff

The board, with the affirmative vote of at least four members, has the authority to hire staff and fix their compensation.[66] Staff is prohibited from engaging in "partisan political activity directly affecting any congressional or presidential election,"[67] and may not "accept public speaking engagements or write for publication on any subject that is in any way related to [their] employment or duties with the Office without specific prior approval from the chairman and cochairman."[68] The board can terminate an employee with an affirmative vote of at least four members.[69] Before staff may begin employment they are required to execute an oath or affirmation on disclosure of information. Copies of the oath or affirmation are provided to the Clerk as part of the records of the House.

The text of the oath is as follows:

> I do solemnly swear (or affirm) that I will not disclose to any person or entity outside of the Office any information received in the course of my service with the Office, except as authorized by the board as necessary to conduct official business or pursuant to its rules.[70]

Staff is required to be impartial and unbiased when conducting an investigation. If a staff member has a conflict of interest arising from "a personal or professional relationship with a subject, a subject's opponent in any election or a witness involved in an investigation, staff shall disclose that fact to the Staff Director who shall disclose it to the Board." If the board determines the investigator cannot be impartial, he or she can be terminated from that investigation.[71]

Powers

The OCE is provided with specific powers to conduct investigations, hold hearings, pay witnesses, and adopt rules. Some of these powers are enumerated in the OCE's authorizing resolution, and others are detailed in rules of conduct to be approved by the OCE.

Investigations

The OCE's primary responsibility is to conduct investigations in an independent, nonpartisan manner, regarding allegations of misconduct against Members, officers, and staff of the House. Following the investigation, the OCE is charged with referring matters, when appropriate, to the Committee on Ethics. Investigations by the OCE are restricted to activities that occurred after March 11, 2008, where a violation of "law, rule, regulation, or other standard of conduct in effect at the time the conduct occurred and [were] applicable to the subject in the performance of his or her duties or the discharge of his or her responsibilities."[72]

Hearings and Evidence

The OCE is authorized to conduct meetings, hold hearings, meet in executive session, solicit testimony, and receive evidence necessary to conduct investigations.[73] Pursuant to OCE rules, documents, recordings, or physical evidence "that was obtained in violation of any law, rule, or regulation" may not be reviewed. To ensure compliance, individuals submitting evidence to the OCE are asked to affirm that the evidence was not obtained in an illegal manner.[74] OCE rules also allow for witnesses and individuals subject to investigation to submit written comments to the OCE. The OCE is also prohibited from considering privileged evidence without a waiver from the House.[75]

Pay Witnesses

The OCE is authorized to pay witnesses in the same manner as prescribed in House Rule XI, clause 5.[76]

OCE Rules

The OCE is authorized to adopt rules necessary to carry out its duties. H.Res. 895 prescribes five rules that the OCE must adopt. These rules cover

- termination of a preliminary review on any ground, including de minimis matters;
- recommendations calling for the Committee on Ethics to dismiss a matter that was subject to a second-phase review on any ground, including being de minimis in nature;
- witness signing statements, acknowledging that the False Statements Act[77] applies to testimony and documents provided to the OCE;
- prohibition of ex parte communications between board members or OCE staff and individuals who are subjects of review or interested parties, and communication between members, officers, or employees of the House with board members or OCE staff regarding matters under review, except as authorized by the board; and
- an OCE code of conduct, which includes the avoidance of conflicts of interest, to govern the behavior of board members and staff.[78]

Information Disclosure

The OCE is required to establish procedures to prevent the unauthorized disclosure of information received by the office. Breaches in confidentiality are to be investigated by the board.[79]

Testimony received or information obtained by the OCE may not be disclosed to any individual or group outside the OCE without the authorization of the board for purposes of conducting official business.[80] Testimony before the Committee on Ethics by board members and staff is exempt from disclosure requirements.[81]

Prior to transmittal of recommendations or statements to the Committee on Ethics, individuals under investigation have the right to present, orally or in writing, a statement on the investigation to the board.[82]

Investigative Procedure

Pursuant to the authority granted by H.Res. 895, Section 1(c)(2)(F), the board is authorized to create an investigatory process to examine and make recommendations on cases brought to the OCE's attention. The process consists of four steps: submission of information, preliminary review, second-phase review, and referral to the Committee on Ethics for further investigation or dismissal of the complaint. Each step, with its authority pursuant to H.Res. 895, and relevant OCE rules are detailed below.

Submission of Information

The OCE was established to conduct independent, nonpartisan reviews of allegations of misconduct by Members, officers, and employees of the House and, when appropriate, to refer matters to the Committee on Ethics under the Rules of the House. Accordingly, it has established procedures for the public to file information alleging wrongdoing and outlines the process for doing so on its website, http://oce.house.gov.

The following should be included in any submission:

1. the name, address, telephone number and e-mail address, if any, of the person submitting the information, and the organization s/he is affiliated with, if any;
2. the full name of the subject of the allegation;
3. the date(s) the alleged conduct occurred;
4. a concise statement of facts (or, the source of the information in the event that the person submitting the information does not have first-hand knowledge of the facts);
5. the law, regulation or rule allegedly violated, if known;
6. if applicable, name(s) and contact information for any potential witness(es);
7. if applicable, copies of any documents related to the allegation; and
8. a signed declaration acknowledging that section 1001 of title 18 United States Code (popularly known as the False Statement Act)

> applies to the information provided. A copy of the False Statements is available on the OCE's website and can be provided on request.
>
> All information will be reviewed by the OCE; however, submitting information does not trigger an investigation. The decision to begin an investigation (preliminary review) lies solely with the Board.83

OCE staff reviews information submitted by the public as well as information derived from other sources, including the press. OCE staff or any board member may submit information for the board's consideration. For an investigation to proceed, at least two board members must concur.

Preliminary Stage Review

The first stage of an investigation is a preliminary review. The preliminary review requires a "*reasonable basis* to believe the allegation based on all the information then known to the board,"[84] the written concurrence of two board members (one appointed by the Speaker and one by the minority leader), and written notification by the board to the Committee on Ethics and the individual subject to the review.[85]

Once a preliminary review has begun, it must be completed within 30 calendar or 5 legislative days, whichever is later, from the receipt of the written request by a minimum of two board members.[86] Prior to, or at the conclusion of, the 30 calendar or 5 legislative days, the board votes on whether to continue the review and advance the inquiry to a second-phase. To continue the review, the board must find "*probable cause* to believe the alleged violation occurred based on all the information then known to the board."[87] An affirmative vote of at least three board members is required to proceed to a second-phase review. If the board does not vote to begin a second-phase investigation by the end of the 30-calendar- or 5-legislative-day time period, the investigation is terminated. The board, however, may vote to terminate an investigation at any time during the preliminary-phase review with the affirmative vote of at least four members.[88]

Regardless of the OCE's decision on proceeding to a second-phase review, the board must notify, in writing, both the Committee on Ethics and the individual under investigation of the board's decision to continue or terminate the investigation. If the board terminates the inquiry, it has the option of sending a report to the Committee on Ethics with its findings.[89]

Second-Phase Review

Should the board vote to conduct a second-phase review, it must be completed within 45 calendar or 5 legislative days, whichever is later.[90] Should the board determine that additional time is needed to conduct the second-phase review, the time period can be extended for an additional 14 calendar days upon a majority vote of the board.[91] This requires the affirmative vote of at least four board members.[92]

When the OCE completes the second-phase review, the board is required to transmit a written report, its findings, if any, and any supporting documentation to the Committee on Ethics.[93] The referrals must be accompanied by two documents: (1) a report which recommends dismissal, further inquiry, or states that the board vote was a tie, and (2) findings. Neither document is to contain conclusions regarding the validity of the allegation or the guilt or innocence of the person subject to the review—such matters are the sole purview of the Committee on Ethics.[94]

The OCE is also obligated to transmit the findings of its investigation, if any, to the Committee on Ethics along with supporting documentation. The findings should include

- findings of fact;
- descriptions of relevant information that was not obtained and witnesses not interviewed;
- recommendations for the issuance of subpoenas; and
- citations of relevant law, rule, regulation, or standard of conduct relevant to the investigation.[95]

The findings should not include the names of cooperative witnesses, any conclusions regarding the validity of the allegations, or statements on the guilt or innocence of the investigative subject.[96] With the findings, the OCE may submit supporting documents,[97] and provide the subject of the investigation a copy of the written report.[98]

Like the House Committee on Ethics, the OCE does not have jurisdiction over former Members of the House. Thus, once a member leaves office, any inquiry or investigation against him or her by either entity will cease in whatever phase a review may be.

The Committee on Ethics and Its Relationship to the OCE

At the conclusion of any second-phase review, the OCE is required to submit a report, and may submit findings and supporting documentation, to the

Committee on Ethics for final disposition.[99] Pursuant to Article 1, Section 5, clause 2 of the Constitution, "[e]ach House may determine the rules of its proceedings, punish its members for disorderly Behaviour, and, with the Concurrence of two thirds, expel a member."[100] For the House of Representatives, this role is delegated to the Committee on Ethics.[101]

Pursuant to House rules, the Committee on Ethics may not receive any referral within 60 days before a federal, state, or local election in which the subject of the case is a candidate.[102] Once the Committee on Ethics receives a referral from the OCE, it must act within 45 days. At that time, the chair must publicly release the committee's actions together with the OCE report and findings, unless the chair and ranking member jointly decide, or the committee votes, to withhold the information for an additional 45 days.[103] The committee is not required to release the OCE findings if it agrees with an OCE decision to dismiss a particular case or chooses to dismiss a case left unresolved by the OCE. The committee does, however, have the option of making the OCE report and findings public.[104]

If the committee decides to take the additional 45 days to consider an OCE referral, at the end of the second 45 days, the chair is required to make public the OCE written report and findings unless the committee votes to initiate an investigation.[105] Should the committee proceed to an investigation, only that fact is announced.[106] The announcement must include the name of the applicable member, officer, or employee, and the alleged violation(s). If the committee deadlocks on a matter referred by the OCE, it must release the OCE's report and findings.[107] At the end of each Congress, any reports and findings not previously related are required to be released.[108] In the event the Committee on Ethics conducts an investigation, it is conducted pursuant to established committee rules.[109] Pursuant to these rules, action on a case may be deferred at the request of law enforcement or regulatory authorities.[110]

Before the Committee on Ethics publicly releases OCE findings and the committee's statement and report, if any, on a referral, the committee is required to give advanced notice of one calendar day to the OCE and any member, officer, or employee who was the subject of a referral.[111]

The Capuano task force envisioned that the Committee on Ethics and the OCE would work closely.[112] The committee is to be notified early and throughout an OCE review.[113] The committee may also ask the OCE to stop a review if the allegation becomes the subject of a Committee on Ethics investigation.[114] In such an occurrence, the OCE board is required to refer the case to the committee, and to treat the matter under the same rules as other OCE referrals. If the committee does not reach a conclusion, it must notify the

OCE board. The OCE board may choose to complete a suspended review.[115] Once a matter is returned to the OCE, it must proceed according to the established process outlined above under "Investigative Procedure."[116]

Referrals to Other Entities

The OCE may also, when appropriate, refer allegations to the Office of Compliance, House Office of the Inspector General, House Commission on Congressional Mail Standards, and state and federal authorities. OCE Rule 13 dictates situations under which referral to one of these entities may be made.

Office of Compliance

Allegations related to laws covered by the Congressional Accountability Act[117] may be referred to the Office of Compliance.[118]

House Office of the Inspector General

Allegations of "fraud, waste and abuse in the operations of the House or joint entities of Congress" may be referred to the Office of the House Inspector General.[119]

House Commission on Congressional Mailing Standards

Allegations "relating to the proper use of the franking privilege" may be referred to the House Commission on Congressional Mailing Standards.[120]

State and Federal Authorities

In consultation with the OCE chair and co-chair, the OCE staff can refer "information to state and federal authorities in the event that information indicates imminent harm or a threat to public safety."[121]

Implementation

Funding

Pursuant to H.Res. 895, the OCE is authorized "such sums as necessary" from applicable accounts of the House.[122] Payments made by the OCE are made on vouchers signed by the chair of the board and approved in the manner directed by the Committee on House Administration. All funds expended by the OCE are subject to regulations prescribed by the Committee on House Administration.[123]

For FY2012, OCE was appropriated $1.548 million.[124] For FY2013, OCE requested the same funding they received in FY2012—$1.548 million.[125] The FY2013 continuing resolution (P.L. 112-175) provided funding for the legislative branch at the FY2012 level, increased by 0.612%, through March 27, 2013.[126] Additionally, appropriations for FY2013 will be considered in the context of the Budget Control Act of 2011 (BCA, P.L. 112-25).[127]

Public Information

Since the OCE was reauthorized in January 2009, the OCE, although not mandated to do so, has issued quarterly reports.[128] Each quarterly report provides a brief summary of OCE activities, including citizen communications, a summary of the OCE process, and a summary of board actions taken during the quarter and for the Congress. *Table 4* provides a summary of the number of cases OCE has considered between 2009 and the third quarter (July to September) 2012.

Table 4. Office of Congressional Ethics Board Action, 2009-2012
Updated through December 31, 2012

	Commence Preliminary Review	*Vote to Terminate Matter*	*Commence Phase II Review*	*Commence Phase II Review Extension*	*Transmit Referral for Review*	*Transmit Referral for Dismissal*
111th Congress						
2009	25	4	21	21	12	8
2010	44	24	20	15	10	10
Total	69	28	41	36	22	18
112th Congress						
2011	22	5	14	10	7	2
2012	10	0	11	9	6	8
Total	32	5	25	19	13	10

Source: CRS Compilation of data summarized in OCE Quarterly Reports (http://oce.house.gov/reports.html).

Notes: Column headers reflect the categories used by the OCE in its quarterly reports. For more information on the stages of review in the headers, see pages 18-22, of this CRS report.

OPTIONS FOR CONGRESS

Creation of the OCE has already changed the relationship between the public and the House ethics process. There are, however, options which might further clarify the OCE's relationship with the public, rank-and-file House members, and the Committee on Ethics. These options each have advantages and disadvantages for the structure of the OCE, its relationship to the Committee on Ethics, and the House's constitutional responsibility to investigate its members. Consequently, careful comparison of all options for the future of the OCE may be useful to ensure that the most effective process is created while ensuring the continued enforcement of House ethics procedures. CRS takes no position on any of the options identified in this report.

Create a Statutory OCE

The OCE exists pursuant to H.Res. 895 (110th Congress) and faces renewal on a biannual basis as part of the House rules package, as was done with the passage of H.Res. 5 in January 2013.[129] Because the OCE operates pursuant to a House resolution, a change in party control or a decision to exclude the OCE from the rules package in a future Congress might result in the elimination of the office.

If the House wanted to ensure the OCE's continuation, it could create a statutory ethics entity. A permanent statutory office would not require reauthorization each Congress. If the House chose to create a statutory office, should the House desire to alter or terminate the program, subsequent legislation would be necessary to amend or terminate the program. Creation of a statutory ethics office, even if only in the House, would require the concurrence of the Senate and the President's signature.

Reform Committee on Ethics to Include Public Outreach

Prior to the creation of the OCE, the Committee on Ethics did not allow public complaints to be to made against Members of Congress.[130] If the House wanted to provide an opportunity for citizens to be involved in the ethics process without the creation of an independent ethics entity (either by resolution or statute), the House could amend House or committee rules to allow the Committee on Ethics to receive formal complaints or information from the general public.

Allowing the public to provide information directly to the Committee on Ethics could allay constitutional concerns over the involvement of an independent entity in investigating and recommending action on internal House enforcement matters. Instead of giving power to an outside entity, the Committee on Ethics could establish mechanisms for the intake and evaluation of citizen complaints prior to investigation and potential action of the full committee. This work could be handled by a subcommittee or by the whole committee.

Should the Committee on Ethics assume this responsibility, the committee's workload could increase substantially. The OCE specifies the number of contacts its staff has with the public and the number of investigations authorized as part of quarterly reports.[131] It is possible that providing the public with direct access to the Committee on Ethics might result in more information (at least at the level currently handled by the OCE) being provided by the public. In addition, a citizen or group providing information might expect the committee to provide updates on the status of investigations.

Amend OCE Authority

The relationship between the OCE and the Committee on Ethics continues to evolve. Under the provisions of H.Res. 895, as the OCE completes second-phase reviews and determines that a further investigation is necessary, the OCE board forwards a report and supporting documentation to the Committee on Ethics.

Subpoena Power

The House could provide the OCE with limited subpoena power to enable the OCE board to conduct more thorough investigations prior to referral to the Committee on Ethics. Providing subpoena power to the OCE might reduce the workload and investigative burden of the Committee on Ethics and prevent duplicative efforts on behalf of the OCE and committee staffs.

Chairman Capuano, in the task force report, explained that consideration was given to empowering the OCE with subpoena power. During the discussions, the task force sought the professional opinion of numerous experts (including the House parliamentarian, House general counsel, and the Congressional Research Service).[132]

The decision not to include subpoena authority was based on various factors, including timeliness.[133] Challenges to a subpoena, it was felt, could hinder and complicate the OCE process and prevent a prompt investigation. Moreover, because of Congress's reluctance to delegate subpoena authority to independent entities, if the task force had recommended giving the OCE that authority, the legislative process might have been delayed while the House debated the merits of the proposal.[134]

Currently, if a subpoena is deemed necessary, the House provides the OCE with the ability to recommend to the Committee on Ethics that a subpoena be issued,[135] as part of the authority already delegated to the committee.[136]

OCE Follow Up

The House could also provide a mechanism whereby the OCE could formally follow up on investigations forwarded to the Committee on Ethics. Pursuant to current practice, the OCE has no recourse to follow a case once it is referred to the committee. Committee rules require that the committee release the OCE report under certain circumstances.[137]

Additional OCE Functions

On March 5, 2009, Representative Ron Paul introduced H.Res. 216. The resolution, if agreed to by the House, would have amended House Rules to require a certain period of time to elapse between introduction of legislation and a vote by the House. Included in the resolutions provisions, Rule XXIX would be amended to allow citizens to petition the board of the Office of Congressional Ethics to investigate potential violations of the new rule.[138]

> Notwithstanding any provision of these rules, any citizen who is eligible to vote and who is not an employee of the executive or judicial branch of the Government may petition the board of the Office of Congressional Ethics to investigate allegations that a member voted for any measure that violated this rule.[139]

The addition to the OCE's jurisdiction by amending House rules could be a way to involve the investigative expertise of the OCE in other House matters. H.Res. 216 implies the OCE's authority to take "complaints" from the general public.[140] This would appear to be incongruent with their current mission to take "information" from public sources and would potentially need to be clarified by the board or by Congress.

Take No Immediate Action

The House might determine that the current relationship between the OCE and the Committee on Ethics is effective. Instead of creating an independent statutory ethics entity, reforming the Committee on Ethics, or amending OCE statute, the House could continue to consider the OCE as part of the rules package in subsequent Congresses. Changes to the OCE could be made on an as-needed basis through House resolutions or through changes to the rules package for subsequent Congresses.

APPENDIX. RULES COMMITTEE AMENDMENTS TO H.RES. 895

Table A-1. Initial and Amended Language Creating the Office of Congressional Ethics

H.Res. 895 as Introduced	Rules Committee Amendments
Appointments made jointly by the Speaker and the minority leader (three designated as Speaker's appointees and three designated as minority leader's appointees) within 90 days of adoption or vacancy. If any position remains vacant beyond 90 days, the appointment shall be made by the Speaker or minority leader, as applicable [sec. 1(b)(1)].	Require that all appointments to the board be made by the Speaker and the minority leader.
N/A	Expand the board to include at least one alternate member from each party.
Require that any two board members needed to initiate a review [sec. 1(c)(1)(A)].	Provide that the OCE reviews be initiated at the request of at least one member appointed by the Speaker and one member appointed by the minority leader.
N/A	Clarify that the board can initiate preliminary reviews.
Second-phase review commences unless the board votes to terminate the	Require the affirmative vote of at least three members to move to a second-phase review.

H.Res. 895 as Introduced	Rules Committee Amendments
preliminary review (with not less than four members voting to terminate) [sec. 1(c)(1)(C)].	
N/A	Provide that if three members do not vote to commence a second-phase review, then the matter is terminated.
N/A	Clarify that subjects of OCE review may make presentations to the board before the board transmits a recommendation or statement to the Committee on Standards of Official Conduct.
N/A	Provide that any time before the end of the preliminary review, four members of the board can vote to terminate it.
N/A	Clarify that members, officers, and staff may not communicate with the OCE regarding OCE cases.
N/A	Impose new confidentiality rules and ex parte communication bars on OCE members and staff.
N/A	Clarify that the elective office agreement pertains also to alternate members and OCE staff but refers only to seeking a seat in the U.S. House or Senate.
N/A	Subject OCE staff to restrictions on political activities.
The committee may not receive any referral from the board of the Office of Congressional Ethics within 60 days before an election in which the subject of the referral is a candidate [sec. 3].	Clarify that the Committee on Standards of Official Conduct may not receive referrals from the OCE within 60 days prior to federal, state, or local elections.

Source: H.Res. 895 (110th Congress), introduced December 19, 2007. U.S. Congress, House, Committee on Rules, Providing for the Adoption of the Resolution (H.Res. 895) Establishing Within the House of Representatives an Office of Congressional Ethics, and for Other Purposes, report to accompany H.Res. 1031, 110th Cong., 2nd sess., March 10, 2008, H.Rept. 110-547 (Washington: GPO, 2008), pp. 2-3.

End Notes

[1] James Madison, "Federalist No. 10, The Same Subject Continued: The Union as a Safeguard Against Domestic Faction and Insurrection," The Federalist Papers, http://thomas.loc.gov/home/histdox/fed_10.html.

[2] Sen. John Cooper et al., "Proposed Amendment of Rule XXV of the Standing Rules of the Senate Relative to the Jurisdiction of the Committee on Rules and Administration," debate in the Senate, Congressional Record, vol. 10, part 13 (July 24, 1964) , pp. 16929-16940. For more information on the Senate Select Committee on Ethics, see CRS Report RL30650, Senate Select Committee on Ethics: A Brief History of Its Evolution and Jurisdiction, by Jacob R. Straus.

[3] Rep. William Colmer et al., "Committee on Standards of Official Conduct," debate in the House, Congressional Record, vol. 113, part. 7 (April 13, 1967), pp. 9426-9448. See also U.S. Congress, House, Committee on Standards of Official Conduct, House Ethics Manual, 110th Cong., 2nd sess. (Washington: GPO, 2008), pp. 4-8; and CRS Report 98- 15, House Committee on Ethics: A Brief History of Its Evolution and Jurisdiction, by Jacob R. Straus.

[4] H.Res. 5 (112th Congress), agreed to January 5, 2011; "Rules of the House" Congressional Record, daily edition, vol. 157 (January 5, 2011), p. H7.

[5] This report does not discuss the ethics process in the Senate, but focuses on the creation of an independent investigatory entity in the House.

[6] Dennis F. Thompson, Overcoming the Conflict of Interest in Congressional Ethics, Woodrow Wilson International Center panel on "Congressional Ethics Enforcement," http://www.wilsoncenter.org/events/docs/ethicsThompson%20paper.pdf, January 16, 2007, pp. 2-3.

[7] Dennis Thompson, "Both Judge and Party, Why Congressional Ethics Committees are Unethical," The Brookings Review, vol. 13, no. 4 (Fall 1995), pp. 44-48. See also, Jack Anderson, "The Embarrassment of Clean Government," June 8, 1975, p. C7; Anthony Marro, "Congressional Ethics and the Need for Basic Reform," The New York Times, January 30, 1977, p. E3; George Lardner, Jr., "Charges of Favoritism, Tests of Credibility at House Ethics Panel," December 15, 1987, p. A21; Ralph Lotkin, "Improving the Ethics Process," Legal Times, February 3, 1997, p. S.36; Eliza Newlin Carney, "Uneasy Umpires," National Journal, May 18, 1996, pp. 1099-1103; Gary Ruskin, "It's Time to Reform Hill Ethics Reform," Roll Call, May 7, 2000, p. 50; Norman Ornstein, "The Senate Is Unable to Police Itself Adequately," Roll Call, March 8, 2006, pp. 6, 8; Fred Wertheimer and Meredith McGehee, "Drain the Swamp Before More End Up Like Ney," Roll Call, March 1, 2007, p. 4; and Editorial, "When Congress Judges Itself, Ethics Fall by the Wayside," USA Today, February 28, 2008, p. 10A.

[8] Don Wolfensberger, Punishing Disorderly Behavior in Congress: The First Century, Woodrow Wilson International Center panel on "Congressional Ethics Enforcement," http://www.wilsoncenter.org/events/docs/ethics-essay-drw.pdf, January 16, 2007, p. 9.

[9] Statement of Office of Congressional Ethics Chair David Skaggs, in U.S. Congress, House, Office of Congressional Ethics, Board Meeting and Public Meeting, 111th Cong., 1st sess., January 23, 2009, (http://oce.house.gov/pdf/ Hearing_on_January_23,_2009.pdf), p. 5.

[10] Ibid.

[11] Ibid. The rules for the Office of Congressional Ethics were amended on February 27, 2009. See U.S. Congress, House, Office of Congressional Ethics, Business Meeting, 111th Cong., 1st sess., February 27, 2009 (http://oce.house.gov/pdf/Hearing_on_February_27,_2009.pdf).

[12] Dennis F. Thompson, Ethics in Congress: From Individual to Institutional Corruption (Washington: The Brookings Institution, 1995), p. 135. Both ethics committees have throughout their existence been criticized as "watchdogs without teeth." See, for example, Robert Sherrill, "We Can't Depend on Congress to Keep Congress Honest," The New York Times Magazine, July 19, 1970, pp. 5-7, 13-14; Jerry Landauer, "Senate Ethics: Hear No Evil, See No Evil," The Washington Star, September 19, 1976, p. E3; Editorial, "Got Ethics?" Roll Call, June 25, 2001, p. 4; Helen Dewar, "Ethics: Can the Senate Police Its Own?" The Washington Post, February 5, 2002, p. A2; Norman Ornstein, "The Senate Is Unable to Police Itself," Roll Call, March 8, 2006, p. 6; Editorial, "Weak Reforms," Roll Call, March 20, 2006, p. 4; and Wilson Abney, "Congressional Ethics: An Evolve or Die Proposition" Roll Call, September 17, 2007, p. 10.

[13] Dennis Thompson, "Both Judge and Party, Why Congressional Ethics Committees are Unethical," The Brookings Review, vol. 13, no. 4 (Fall 1995), pp. 44-48. See also footnote 7.

[14] For a selected list of legislative proposals see Table 1 and Table 2. See also Dennis Thompson, "Both Judge and Party, Why Congressional Ethics Committees are Unethical," The Brookings Review, vol. 13, no. 4 (Fall 1995), pp. 44- 48; John Gregg, "Independent Board to Police Members?" Roll Call, August 21, 1988, pp. 3, 18; Glenn Simpson, "Non-Senators Proposed to Be Ethics Panelists," Roll Call, October 8, 1991, pp. 1, 27; Norman Ornstein, "Put Congressmen Emeriti on Ethics Panels," Wall Street Journal, May 28, 1991, p. A22; Juliet Eilperin, "Debate Joined Over Outside Ethics Panel for House," Roll Call, February 10, 1997, p. 10; Norman Ornstein, "Use Former Members, Staff to Filter Ethics Complaints," Roll Call, February 4, 2004, p. 6; and Editorial, "Locking Up the Ghost of Congress Past," The New York Times, March 3, 2007, p. A26.

[15] Sen. William Roth, remarks in the Senate, Congressional Record, vol. 126 (February 6, 1980), pp. 2099-2100. Senator Roth was discussing S.J.Res. 144, his proposal to establish an Independent Commission on Ethics to conduct investigations of allegations of improper conduct by members of Congress connected with the so-called ABSCAM scandal.

[16] Dennis Thompson, "Both Judge and Party, Why Congressional Ethics are Unethical," The Brookings Review, vol. 13, no. 4 (Fall 1995), p. 45. See also, Dennis F. Thompson, Ethics in Congress: From Individual to Institutional Corruption (Washington: The Brookings Institution, 1995); Dennis F. Thompson, Political Ethics and Public Office (Cambridge, MA: Harvard University Press, 1990); and Dennis F. Thompson, Restoring Responsibility: Ethics in Government, Business, and Healthcare (New York: Cambridge University Press, 2004).

[17] Sen. J. William Fulbright, "Commission on Ethics in Government," remarks in the Senate, Congressional Record, vol. 97, part 3 (March 28, 1951), p. 2938.

[18] U.S. Congress, Senate, Committee on Labor and Human Resources, Subcommittee to Study Senate Concurrent Resolution 21, Establishment of a Commission on Ethics in Government, hearings , 82nd Cong., 1st sess., June 19, 1951 (Washington: GPO, 1951), p. 2.

[19] U.S. Congress, Senate, Committee on Labor and Public Welfare, Special Subcommittee on the Establishment of a Commission on Ethics in Government, Ethical Standards in Government: Proposals for Improvement of Ethical Standards in the Federal Government Including Establishment of a Commission on Ethics in Government, committee print, 82nd Cong., 1st sess. (Washington: GPO, 1951), pp. 1-2.

[20] 5 U.S.C. §§511-599.

[21] U.S. Congress, Senate, Committee on Labor and Public Welfare, Special Subcommittee on the Establishment of a Commission on Ethics in Government, Ethical Standards in Government: Proposals for Improvement of Ethical Standards in the Federal Government Including Establishment of a Commission on Ethics in Government, committee print, 82nd Cong., 1st sess. (Washington: GPO, 1951), pp. 2-4.

[22] U.S. Congress, Joint Committee on the Organization of Congress, Ethics Process: Testimony of Former Senator Abraham A. Ribicoff and a Panel of Academic Experts, 103rd Cong., 1st sess., February 16, 1993, S.Hrg. 103-13 (Washington: GPO, 1993); U.S. Congress, Joint Committee on the Organization of Congress, Ethics Process: Testimony of Hon. Howell Heflin; Hon. Trent Lott; Hon. Henry J. Hyde; Hon. Curt Weldon; and Hon. Robert E. Andrews, 103rd Cong., 1st sess., February 23, 1993, S.Hrg. 103-37 (Washington: GPO, 1993); and U.S. Congress, Joint Committee on the Organization of Congress, Ethics

Process: Testimony of Hon. Louis Stokes, Hon. James Hansen, and a Panel of Academic Experts, 103rd Cong., 1st sess., February 25, 1993, S.Hrg. 103-14 (Washington: GPO, 1993).

[23] U.S. Congress, Joint Committee on the Organization of Congress, Organization of the Congress. Final Report of the Senate Members of the Joint Committee on the Organization of Congress, 103rd Cong., 1st sess., S.Rept. 103-215, vol. 1 (Washington: GPO, 1993), p. 21.

[24] U.S. Congress, Joint Committee on the Organization of Congress, Organization of the Congress. Final Report of the House Members of the Joint Committee on the Organization of Congress, 103rd Cong., 1st sess., H.Rept. 103-413, vol. 1 (Washington: GPO, 1993), pp. 12-13.

[25] For more information on the hearings and background of ethics issues in Congress, see U.S. Congress, Joint Committee on the Organization of Congress, Background Materials: Supplemental Information Provided to Members of the Joint Committee on the Organization of Congress, committee print, 103rd Cong., 1st sess., S.Prt. 103-55 (Washington: GPO, 1993), pp. 115-165.

[26] U.S. Congress, Speaker of the House, "Pelosi Announces Special Task Force on Ethics Enforcement," press release, January 31, 2007, http://speaker.house.gov/newsroom/pressreleases?id=0057. The other members of the task force were Representative Bobby Scott, Representative Marty Meehan, Representative Betty McCollum, Representative Lamar Smith (ranking member), Representative Dave Camp, Representative Dave Hobson, and Representative Todd Tiahrt. Representative David Price was appointed to the task force in July 2007 when Representative Meehan resigned from Congress.

[27] U.S. Congress, House, Special Task Force on Ethics Enforcement, Report of the Democratic Members of the Special Task Force on Ethics Enforcement, committee print, 110th Cong., 1st sess., H.Prt. 110-1 (Washington: GPO, 2007), pp. 4-5. [Hereafter, Task Force Democratic Members Report].

[28] U.S. Congress, Speaker of the House, "Pelosi: Democrats' First Order of Business in the New Congress Will Be Ethics Reform," press release, November 27, 2006. A copy of the press release is available by request from the author.

[29] U.S. Congress, Senate, Office of Majority Leader Harry Reid, "Democrats Pledge to Provide Honest Leadership, Open Government," press release, January 18, 2006, http://democrats .senate.gov/newsroom/record.cfm?id=250503&.

[30] Public Citizen, "Six Benchmarks for Lobbying Reform," Congress Watch, January 26, 2006, http://www.citizen.org/ congress/govt_reform/_government_/articles.cfm?ID=14877.

[31] "CNN/USAToday/Galllup Poll," USA Today, January 6-8, 2006, http://www.usatoday. com/ news/polls/2006-01-09- poll.htm.

[32] U.S. Congress, House, Special Task Force on Ethics Enforcement, Public Hearing on Ethics Process, 110th Cong., 1st sess., April 19, 2007 (http://www.house.gov/capuano/ news/2007 /121907ethics/Hearing%20Transcript%20- %20working.pdf), p. 2. [Hereafter, Task Force Public Hearing].

[33] Ibid., p. 7.

[34] Testimony of Judicial Watch President Tom Fitton, in Task Force Public Hearing, (http://www.house.gov/capuano/news/2007/121907ethics/Witness%20Testimony%20-%20 Fitton.pdf) p. 2.

[35] Testimony of Woodrow Wilson International Center for Scholars Congress Project Director Don Wolfensbeger, in Task Force Public Hearing, (http://www.house.gov/capuano/ news/2007/121907ethics/Hearing%20Transcript%20- %20working.pdf).

[36] Ibid., pp. 3-4.

[37] Letter from Representative Zack Space, Representative Baron Hill, Representative Nick Lampson, Representative Bruce Braley, Representative Michael Arcuri, Representative David Loebsack, Representative Jason Altmire, Representative Ed Perlmutter, Representative Nancy Boyda, Representative Timothy Walz, Representative Tim Mahoney, Representative Gabrielle Giffords, Representative Christopher Murphy, Representative Kristen Gillibrand, Representative Paul Hodes, Representative Joe Courtney, Representative Jerry McNerney, Representative Brad Ellsworth, Representative Steve Kagen, Representative Carol Shea-Porter, Representative Ron Klein, Representative Betty Sutton, Representative John Yarmuth, Representative Patrick Murphy, Representative Phil Hare, Representative Joe Sestak, and Representative John Hall, to Chairman Michael Capuano, Special Task Force on Ethics Enforcement, April 23, 2007. A copy of the letter is available from the author.

[38] Task Force Democratic Members Report, p. III.

[39] Ibid., pp. 1-2.

[40] Ibid., p. 6.

[41] Rep. Michael Capuano, "Congressman Mike Capuano Releases Report of the Special Task Force on Ethics Enforcement," press release, December 19, 2007, http://www.house.gov /capuano/news/2007/pr121907.shtml. See also, Dear Colleague Letter from Representative Michael Capuano, chair, Special Task Force on Ethics Enforcement, December 19, 2007 (http://www.house.gov/capuano/news/2007/ 121907ethics/Dear%20 Colleague%20Letter.pdf).

[42] Dear Colleague Letter from Representative Michael Capuano, chair, Special Task Force on Ethics Enforcement, "AMENDMENTS to the Proposed Reforms to the ETHICS PROCESS," March 3, 2008 (http://www.house.gov/ capuano/news/2008/pr121907-letter030308.pdf).

[43] Rep. Michael Capuano, "Opinion-Editorial: Time to Pass an Ethics Reform Bill With an Independent Board," press release, March 5, 2008, http://www.house.gov/capuano/ news/ 2008/oe030508.shtml.

[44] U.S. Congress, House, Committee on Rules, Providing for the Adoption of the Resolution (H.Res. 895) Establishing Within the House of Representatives an Office of Congressional Ethics, and for Other Purposes, report to accompany H.Res. 1031, 110th Cong., 2nd sess., March 10, 2008, H.Rept. 110-547 (Washington: GPO, 2008), p. 1.

[45] Rep. Betty Sutton et al., "Establishing an Office of Congressional Ethics," House debate, Congressional Record, daily edition, vol. 154 (March 11, 2008), pp. H1515-H1535.

[46] Rep. Michael Capuano, "Congressman Mike Capuano's Statement on the Passage of H.Res. 895, Establishing an Independent Office of Congressional Ethics," press release, March 11, 2008, http://www.house.gov/capuano/news/ 2008/st031108.shtml.

[47] H.Res. 5, §4(d) (113th Congress), agreed to January 3, 2013; "Rules of the House" Congressional Record, daily edition, vol. 159 (January 3, 2013), p. H6.

[48] H.Res. 895 §1(b)(6)(A).

[49] H.Res. 895 §1(b)(1).

[50] H.Res. 895 §1(b)(6)(C). H.Res. 895 does not provide a direct definition of dismissal for cause. For executive branch definitions see 5 U.S.C. §4303 on unacceptable performance, chapter 75 of Title 5 United States Code on adverse actions, 5 C.F.R. §752.401 et seq. on implementing regulations, and 5 C.F.R. §752.403 on standards for action by an employing authority.

[51] H.Res. 895 §1(b)(8). H.Res. 895 establishes quorum as a majority of members of the board.

[52] H.Res. 895 §1(b)(6)(A).

[53] H.Res. 5 (113th Congress), §4(d)(3)(4-)

[54] H.Res. 895 §1(k)(2).

[55] H.Res. 895 §1(k)(1).

[56] H.Res. 895 §1(f)(1)(A).

[57] H.Res. 895 §1(b)(3).

[58] H.Res. 895 §1(b)(8).

[59] H.Res. 895 §1(b)(2).

[60] H.Res. 895 §1(b)(4)(A).

[61] P.L. 104-65, 109 Stat. 691, December 19, 1995, as amended by P.L. 105-166, 112 Stat. 38, April 8, 1998; and P.L. 110-81, 121 Stat. 735, September 14, 2007. For more information on the Lobbying Disclosure Act, see CRS Report R40245, Lobbying Registration and Disclosure: Before and After the Enactment of the Honest Leadership and Open Government Act of 2007, by Jacob R. Straus; CRS Report RL34377, Lobbying Registration and Disclosure: The Role of the Clerk of the House and the Secretary of the Senate, by Jacob R. Straus; and CRS Report RL31126, Lobbying Congress: An Overview of Legal Provisions and Congressional Ethics Rules, by Jack Maskell.

[62] 22 U.S.C. §611 et seq. The Department of Justice maintains the Foreign Agents Registration Unit. More information can be found on the FARA website at http://www.usdoj.gov/criminal/fara/.

[63] H.Res. 895 §1(b)(4)(B)(i)(I)-(VI).

[64] H.Res. 895 §1(b)(4)(B)(ii).

[65] H.Res. 895 §1(b)(7).

[66] H.Res. 895 §1(h).

[67] H.Res. 895 §1(k)(3)(D).

[68] H.Res. 895 §1(k)(3)(E).

[69] H.Res. 895 §1(i).

[70] H.Res. 895 §1(f)(1)(A).

[71] U.S. Congress, House, Office of Congressional Ethics, "Rule 5. Investigator is Impartial," Rules for the Conduct of Investigations, 111th Cong., 1st sess. (http://oce.house.gov/pdf/20090127_rules_as_adopted.pdf), p. 9. [Hereafter, OCE Investigations Rules].

[72] OCE Investigations Rules, "Introduction," p. 1.

[73] H.Res. 895 §1(c)(2)(D).

[74] OCE Investigations Rules, "Rule 4. Evidence," p. 8.

[75] Ibid. The OCE's policy is to follow the same privileges the House recognizes. Meeting between the authors and Leo Wise, staff director and chief counsel, Office of Congressional Ethics, July 15, 2009.

[76] H.Res. 895 §1(c)(2)(E). House Rules XI, clause 5 states "Witnesses appearing before the House or any of its committees shall be paid the same per diem rate as established, authorized, and regulated by the Committee on House Administration for Members, Delegates, the Resident Commissioner, and employees of the House, plus actual expenses of travel to or from the place of examination. Such per diem may not be paid when a witness has been summoned at the place of examination." See also U.S. Congress, House, "Rules XI, clause 5," Rules of the House of Representatives One Hundred Eleventh Congress, prepared by Lorraine C. Miller, Clerk of the House of Representatives, 111th Cong., 1st sess., January 28, 2009 (http://www.rules.house.gov/ruleprec/111th.pdf). [Hereafter, House Rules].

[77] 18 U.S.C. §1001.

[78] H.Res. 895 §1(c)(2)(F)(i)-(iv).
[79] H.Res. 895 §1(f)(1)(C).
[80] H.Res. 895 §1(f)(1)(B).
[81] H.Res. 895 §1(f)(2).
[82] H.Res. 895 §1(f)(3).
[83] OCE Investigations Rules, p. 6; and U.S. Congress, House, Office of Congressional Ethics, "How to Submit Information to the OCE," About-Office of Congressional Ethics (http://www.oce.house.gov/ how_to_submit_info.shtml).
[84] OCE Investigations Rules, "Rule 7. Preliminary Review," p. 10. Pursuant to OCE rule seven, a reasonable basis "to believe an allegation exists when there is a reasonable and articulate basis for believing the allegation."
[85] H.Res. 895 §1(c)(1)(A).
[86] H.Res. 895 §1(c)(1)(B).
[87] OCE Investigations Rules, "Rule 8. Second-Phase Review," p. 12. Pursuant to OCE rule eight, probable cause "exists if the evidence is sufficient to lead a person of ordinary caution and prudence to believe or entertain a strong suspicion that a Member, officer or employee committed a violation."
[88] H.Res. 895 §1(c)(1)(C).
[89] H.Res. 895 §1(c)(1)(C).
[90] H.Res. 895 §1(c)(2)(A)(i).
[91] H.Res. 895 §1(c)(2)(A)(ii).
[92] H.Res. 895 §1(c)(2)(B).
[93] H.Res. 895 §1(c)(2)(C).
[94] H.Res. 895 §1(c)(2)(C)(i)(I)(aa)-(cc). See also Rep. Michael Capuano, "Summary of H.Res. 895: Establishing within the House of Representatives an Office of Congressional Ethics," press release, March 10, 2008, http://www.house.gov/capuano/news/2008/up031008.shtml. If the OCE finds that there is "substantial reason to believe the allegations," the matter must be referred to the Committee on Standards of Official Conduct. Substantial reason "exists where there is such relevant evidence a reasonable mind might accept as adequate to support a conclusion." See also OCE Investigations Rules, "Rule 9. Referrals to the Standards Committee," p. 13.
[95] H.Res. 895 §1(c)(2)(C)(i)(II)(aa)-(cc).
[96] H.Res. 895 §1(c)(2)(C)(i)(II)(dd).
[97] H.Res. 895 §1(c)(2)(C)(i)(III).
[98] H.Res. 895 §1(c)(2)(C)(ii). The copy provided to the subject of the investigation is a statement of the nature of the report and the board vote.
[99] H.Res. 895 §1(c)(2)(C), and Task Force Democratic Members Report, pp. 14-18.
[100] U.S. Congress, House, The Constitution of the United States, 108th Cong., 1st sess., H.Doc. 108-96 (Washington: GPO, 2003), p. 4.
[101] House Rules, Rule XI, clause 3. See also CRS Report 98-15, House Committee on Ethics: A Brief History of Its Evolution and Jurisdiction, by Jacob R. Straus.
[102] House Rules, Rule XI, clause 3 (b)(8)(D).
[103] Task Force Democratic Members Report, p. 15, and House Rules, Rule XI clause 3(b)(8). Receipt of a report by the committee from the OCE automatically bypasses the committee's Rule 16(a) for what constitutes a complaint.
[104] Task Force Democratic Members Report, p. 15.
[105] House Rules, Rule XI, clause 3 (b)(8)(B)(iii).

[106] The OCE report and findings are not to be released until after completion of the process pursuant to committee rules unless the investigative subcommittee does not conclude within a year. The committee is also required to make OCE findings public at the end of a Congress pursuant to House Rules, Rule XI, clause 3 (b)(8)(B)(iii).

[107] Task Force Democratic Members Report, p. 16.

[108] Meeting with Omar Ashmay, staff director and general counsel, Office of Congressional Ethics, 2012.

[109] U.S. Congress, House, Committee on Ethics, Rules, 112th Cong., 2nd sess., December 18, 2012, at (http://ethics.house.gov/sites/ethics.house.gov/files/ Committee%20Rules%20for%20112th%20Congress%20as%20amended%20December%2018%202012.pdf). See also, Task Force Democratic Members Report, p. 16.

[110] Task Force Democratic Members Report, p. 16, and Ethics Committee Rules 15(f).

[111] House Rules, Rule XI, clause 3 (b)(8)(A).

[112] Task Force Democratic Members Report, p. 17.

[113] Ibid.

[114] Ibid., and OCE Investigations Rules, "Rule 12. Requests from the Standards Committee," pp. 16-17.

[115] Ibid.

[116] Ibid.

[117] P.L. 104-1, 109 Stat. 3, January 23, 1995. The Congressional Accountability Act (CAA) of 1995, as enacted, applied 11 civil rights, labor, and workplace safety and health laws to the U.S. Congress and its associated agencies, from which it had previously been exempt. See also Office of Compliance, "What is the CAA?" http://www.compliance.gov/covered/popups/whatis.htm. The laws are, the Age Discrimination in Employment Act of 1967 (29 U.S.C. §621 et seq.); the Americans with Disabilities Act of 1990 (42 U.S.C. §12101 et seq.); Title VII of the Civil Rights Act of 1964 (42 U.S.C. §2000e et seq.); the Employee Polygraph Protection Act of 1988 (29 U.S.C. §2001 et seq.); the Fair Labor Standards Act of 1938 (29 U.S.C. §201 et seq.); the Family and Medical Leave Act of 1993 (29 U.S.C. §2611 et seq.); the Federal Service Labor Management Relations Statute (Title 5, Chapter 71 U.S. Code); the Occupational Safety and Health Act of 1970 (29 U.S.C. §651 et seq.); the Rehabilitation Act of 1973 (29 U.S.C. §701 et seq.); and the Veteran's employment and reemployment rights (Title 38, Chapter 43 U.S. Code); and Worker Adjustment and Retraining Notification Act (29 U.S.C. §2101 et seq.).

[118] OCE Investigation Rules, "Rule 13. Referrals to Other Entities," p. 17.

[119] Ibid. For more information on the Office of the House Inspector General, see CRS Report R40133, Office of the House of Representatives Inspector General, by Jacob R. Straus.

[120] Ibid. For more information on the Franking Privilege or the House Commission on Congressional Mailing Standards, see CRS Report RL34274, Franking Privilege: Historical Development and Options for Change, by Matthew Eric Glassman, CRS Report RL34458, Franking Privilege: Mass Mailings and Mass Communications in the House, 1997-2011, by Matthew Eric Glassman; and CRS Report RS22771, Congressional Franking Privilege: Background and Recent Legislation, by Matthew Eric Glassman.

[121] Ibid., p. 18.

[122] The Office of Congressional Ethics is funded through Legislative Branch appropriations from the "Allowances and Expenses" account for the House of Representatives. For more information on Legislative Branch Appropriations, see CRS Report R41870, Legislative Branch: FY2012 Appropriations, by Ida A. Brudnick; and CRS Report R42500, Legislative Branch: FY2013 Appropriations, by Ida A. Brudnick.

[123] H.Res. 895 §1(l).

[124] P.L. 112-74, 125 Stat. 1120, December 23, 2011.

[125] Office of Management and Budget, Appendix, Budget of the United States Government, FY2013 (Washington: GPO, 2012), pp. 17-49.

[126] H.J.Res. 117, P.L. 112-175, September 28, 2012. For additional information on the FY2013 continuing resolution, see CRS Report R42782, FY2013 Continuing Resolution: Analysis of Components and Congressional Action, by Jessica Tollestrup. For additional information on continuing resolutions generally, see CRS Report R42647, Continuing Resolutions: Overview of Components and Recent Practices, by Jessica Tollestrup.

[127] For information on the OCE in the OMB Report Pursuant to the Sequestration Transparency Act of 2012 (P.L. 112- 155), see Appendix A. Preliminary Estimates of Sequestrable and Exempt Budgetary Resources and Reduction in Sequestrable Budgetary Resources by OMB Account - FY 2013 and Appendix B. Preliminary Sequestrable / Exempt Classification by OMB Account and Type of Budgetary Resource, in Available at http://www.whitehouse.gov/sites/ default/files/omb/assets/legislative_reports/stareport.pdf. For additional information, see CRS Report R41965, The Budget Control Act of 2011, by Bill Heniff Jr., Elizabeth Rybicki, and Shannon M. Mahan; and CRS Report R42050, Budget "Sequestration" and Selected Program Exemptions and Special Rules, coordinated by Karen Spar.

[128] Copies of the OCEs quarterly reports can be found at http://oce.house.gov/reports.html.

[129] H.Res. 5 (113th Congress), agreed to January 3, 2013; "Rules of the House" Congressional Record, daily edition, vol. 159 (January 3, 2013), p. H6.

[130] The Committee on Ethics allowed public complaints prior to 1997. In 1997, the Bi-Partisan House Ethics Task Force recommended changes to the House ethics rules that prohibited public complaints. For more information see Rep. Gerald Solomon, "Providing for Consideration of H.Res. 168, Implementing the Recommendations of the BiPartisan House Ethics Reform Task Force," Congressional Record, vol. 143, part 13 (September 18, 1997), pp. 19302- 19340; and CRS Report 98-15, House Committee on Ethics: A Brief History of Its Evolution and Jurisdiction, by Jacob R. Straus.

[131] U.S. Congress, House, Office of Congressional Ethics, Quarterly Report: January to March 2009, 111th Cong., 1st sess., March 2009; and U.S. Congress, House, Office of Congressional Ethics, Quarterly Report: April - June 2009, 111th Cong., 1st sess., July 13, 2009.

[132] Task Force Democratic Members Report, pp. 13-14. "Indirect" subpoena power refers to a subpoena issued by the House Committee on Ethics on behalf of the OCE. Several measures were introduced in the House in the 110th Congress calling for some form of an independent ethics commission with subpoena power. See, for example, H.R. 1136, H.R. 1754, H.R. 2544, H.R. 2822, H.R. 4239, and H.Res. 1018.

[133] Task Force Democratic Members Report, pp. 13-14.

[134] Ibid., p. 14.

[135] Ibid.

[136] U.S. Congress, House, Committee on Standards of Official Conduct, Rules, 111th Cong., 1st sess., June 9, 2009 (http://ethics.house.gov/Media/PDF/ 111th_Rules_ Amended_June_ 2009.pdf), p. 17.

[137] House Rules, Rule XI, clause 3 (b)(8)(B)(iii).

[138] House Rule XXIX in clause 1 applies the rules of the previous Congress to the current Congress, as applicable, and states that the "rules of parliamentary practice comprised by Jefferson's Manual shall govern the House in all cases to which they are applicable and in

which they are not inconsistent with the Rules and orders of the House." Clause 2 clarifies the use of words "imparting one gender" apply to the other gender as well. For more information, see House Rules XXIX.

[139] H.Res. 216, introduced March 5, 2009.

[140] Should the House decide to allow the public to submit complaints directly to the OCE, one option might be to require individuals who want to submit material to do so by making a sworn complaint. For example, on May 28, 2010, Representative Marcia Fudge introduced H.Res. 1416 to amend the Rules of the House "regarding the public disclosure by the Committee on Standards of Official Conduct of written reports and findings of the board of the Office of Congressional Ethics.... " Among other items, the resolution would amend Rule XI, clause 3(b)(8) to change reporting requirements for OCE reports and make changes to the OCE inquiry process surrounding "sworn complaint[s] from a citizen asserting personal knowledge of any alleged violation by that Member, officer, or employee of any law, rule, regulation, or other standard of conduct applicable to such individual in the performance of his duties or the discharge of his responsibilities."

In: U.S. House of Representatives
Editor: Bruno Montagne

ISBN: 978-1-62808-364-4

Chapter 3

EXPULSION, CENSURE, REPRIMAND, AND FINE: LEGISLATIVE DISCIPLINE IN THE HOUSE OF REPRESENTATIVES*

Jack Maskell

SUMMARY

The House of Representatives—in the same manner as the United States Senate—is expressly authorized within the United States Constitution (Article I, Section 5, clause 2) to discipline or "punish" its own Members. This authority of the House to discipline a Member for "disorderly Behaviour" is in addition to any criminal or civil liability that a Member of the House may incur for particular misconduct, and is used not merely to punish an individual Member, but to protect the institutional integrity of the House of Representatives, its proceedings, and its reputation.

The House may discipline its Members without the necessity of Senate concurrence. The most common forms of discipline in the House are now "expulsion," "censure," or "reprimand"; although the House may also discipline its Members in other ways, including fine or monetary restitution, loss of seniority, and suspension or loss of certain privileges. In addition to such sanctions imposed by the full House of

* This is an edited, reformatted and augmented version of a Congressional Research Service publication, CRS Report for Congress RL31382, prepared for Members and Committees of Congress, from www.crs.gov, dated May 2, 2013.

Representatives, the standing committee in the House which deals with ethics and official conduct matters, the House Committee on Ethics—formerly called the Committee on Standards of Official Conduct—is authorized by House Rules to issue a formal "Letter of Reproval" for misconduct which does not rise to the level of consideration or sanction by the entire House of Representatives. Additionally, the Committee on Ethics has also expressed its disapproval of certain conduct in informal letters and communications to Members.

The House may generally discipline its Members for violations of statutory law, including crimes; for violations of internal congressional rules; or for any conduct which the House of Representatives finds has reflected discredit upon the institution. Thus, each house of Congress has disciplined its own Members for conduct which has not necessarily violated any specific rule or law, but which was found to breach its privileges, demonstrate contempt for the institution, or reflect discredit on the House or Senate. When the most severe sanction of expulsion has been employed in the House of Representatives, however, the underlying conduct deemed by the House to have merited removal from office has historically involved either disloyalty to the United States Government, or the violation of a criminal law involving the abuse of one's official position, such as bribery. The House of Representatives has actually expelled only five Members in its history, but a number of Members, facing likely congressional discipline for various forms of misconduct, have resigned from Congress prior to any formal House action or leave office after election defeat.

Background

Each house of the United States Congress is expressly authorized within the Constitution to "punish" its own Members for misconduct. In imposing legislative discipline against its Members, the House operates through its rulemaking powers,[1] and the express provision for legislative discipline is set out along with Congress' rulemaking authority in Article I, Section 5, clause 2, of the Constitution:

> Each House may determine the Rules of its Proceedings, punish its Members for disorderly Behaviour, and, with the Concurrence of two thirds, expel a Member.

The underlying justification for legislative discipline has traditionally been to protect the integrity and dignity of the legislature and its proceedings, rather than merely to punish an individual;[2] and such internal legislative process is *additional* to any potential criminal or civil liability that a Member might incur for any particular misconduct.[3] Members of Congress, like any other persons in the United States, are subject generally to outside law enforcement and criminal prosecution if their misconduct constitutes a violation of federal, state, or local criminal law. Unlike members of the legislatures or parliaments of many foreign nations, there is *no* general immunity from all criminal prosecution for Members of the United States Congress during their tenure in office. Rather, Members of Congress have a fairly narrow (although complete) immunity from outside prosecution for "Speech or Debate" in either house of Congress.[4]

Members of the House of Representatives are subject to internal, congressional discipline for any conduct which the institution of the House believes warrants such discipline. The express constitutional authority drafted by the framers of the Constitution was drawn from the British parliamentary practice, as well as from our own colonial legislative experience, and reflects the principle and understanding that although the qualifications of Members of Congress were intentionally kept to a minimum to allow the voters the broadest discretion in sending whomever they please to represent them in Congress,[5] the institution of the House has the right to discipline those who breach its privileges or decorum, or who damage its integrity or reputation, even to the extent of expelling from Congress a duly-elected Member.[6]

Internal, congressional discipline of a Member may take several forms. The most common forms of discipline in the House of Representatives are now "expulsion," "censure," or "reprimand," although the House may also discipline its Members in other ways, including fine or monetary assessment, loss of seniority, or loss of certain privileges.[7] An "expulsion" is a removal of a Member from the House of Representatives by a two-thirds vote of the House. A "censure" or a "reprimand" is a legislative procedure where the full House, by majority vote on a simple resolution, expresses a formal disapproval of the conduct of a Member. In addition to these punishments or disciplines by the entire House of Representatives, the House Committee on Ethics—formerly called the Committee on Standards of Official Conduct—is authorized to issue, on its own accord, a "Letter of Reproval" to a Member when that committee disapproves of conduct but makes no recommendation for legislative sanctions to the full House of Representatives. The committee has also from time-to-time expressed its disapproval of particular conduct in informal letters and other communications to Members.

There is no precise listing or description in the Rules of the House of Representatives of the specific types of misconduct or ethical improprieties which might subject a Member to the various potential disciplines. The Rules adopted by the House Committee on Ethics provide simply that:

> With respect to the sanctions that the Committee may recommend, reprimand is appropriate for serious violations, censure is appropriate for more serious violations, and expulsion of a Member or dismissal of an officer or employee is appropriate for the most serious violations. A recommendation of a fine is appropriate in a case in which it is likely that the violation was committed to secure a personal financial benefit; and a recommendation of a denial or limitation of a right, power, privilege, or immunity of a Member is appropriate when the violation bears upon the exercise or holding of such right, power, privilege, or immunity.[8]

The House may discipline its Members for violations of statutory law, including crimes; for violations of internal congressional rules; or for any conduct which the House of Representatives finds has reflected discredit upon the institution.[9] Each house of Congress has disciplined its own Members for conduct which has not necessarily violated any specific rule or law, but which was found to breach its privileges, demonstrate contempt for the institution, or which was found to discredit the House or Senate.[10] When the most severe sanction of expulsion has been employed or recommended in the House, however, the conduct has historically involved either disloyalty to the United States Government, or the violation of a criminal law involving the abuse of one's official position, such as bribery.

EXPULSION

Expulsion is the form of action by which the House of Representatives, after a Member has taken the oath of office, removes that Representative from membership in the body by a vote of two-thirds of the Members present and voting.[11] An expulsion is considered a disciplinary matter and a matter of self-protection of the integrity of the institution and its proceedings, and as such is substantively and procedurally different from an "exclusion," which denies a Member-elect his or her seat by a simple *majority* vote of the body, prior to the Member-elect being seated (or after being seated "without prejudice" pending investigation and resolution of the matter), because of failure of the

Member-elect to meet the constitutional qualifications for office (*i.e.*, age, citizenship and inhabitancy in the state from which elected), or because of a failure to have been "duly elected"; an "exclusion" is now understood *not* to be a disciplinary procedure.[12] A Member is "expelled" by a two-thirds vote, however, precisely for issues of misconduct, and expulsion is generally taken against a Member after the Member has been sworn into office.

Members of the United States Congress are not removed by way of an "impeachment" procedure in the legislature, as are executive and judicial officers, but are subject to the more simplified and expedited legislative process of expulsion.[13] A removal through an impeachment, it should be noted, requires the action of both houses of Congress—impeachment in the House and trial and conviction in the Senate. An expulsion, however, is accomplished merely by the House or Senate acting alone concerning one of its own Members, without the consent or action of the other body, and without the constitutional requirement of trial and conviction.[14]

Grounds for Expulsion

There is no limitation apparent on the face of the Constitution, nor in the deliberations of the Framers, on the authority to expel a Member of Congress, other than the two-thirds vote requirement. One study of the expulsion clause summarized the Framers' intent as follows:

> [From] the history of Article I, Section 5, clause 2, and in particular its course in the Committee of Detail, it is clear that the Framers ... did not intend to impose any limitation on Congressional power to determine what conduct warranted expulsion.... Nor do the debates in the Convention suggest any desire to impose any other substantive restrictions on the expulsion power.[15]

Justice Joseph Story similarly concluded that it would be "difficult to draw a clear line of distinction between the right to inflict the punishment of expulsion, and any other punishment upon a member, founded on the time, place, or nature or the offense," and that "expulsion may be for any misdemeanor, which, though not punishable by any statute, is inconsistent with the trust and duty of" a Member.[16]

The Supreme Court of the United States, citing Justice Story's historic treatise on the Constitution, found an expansive authority and discretion within each house of Congress concerning the grounds for expulsion. In *In re Chapman*, the Supreme Court noted the Senate expulsion case of Senator William Blount[17] as supporting the constitutional authority of either house of Congress to punish a Member for conduct which in the judgment of the body "is inconsistent with the trust and duty of a member" even if such conduct was "not a statutable offense nor was it committed in his official character, nor was it committed during the session of Congress, nor at the seat of government."[18] While each house of Congress has broad authority as to the grounds for an expulsion, this disciplinary action is generally understood to be reserved only for the "most serious violations."[19] As noted above, expulsions in the House (and in the Senate) have traditionally involved conduct which implicated disloyalty to the Union, or the commission of a crime involving the abuse of one's office or authority.

Precedents and Practice

The House of Representatives has actually expelled only five Members (four Members and one Member-elect) in its history, three of whom were expelled during the Civil War period in 1861 for disloyalty to the Union.[20] The fourth Member of the House to be expelled was Representative Michael J. (Ozzie) Myers, of Pennsylvania, on October 2, 1980, after his bribery conviction for receiving a payment in return for promising to use official influence on immigration bills in the so-called ABSCAM "sting operation" run by the FBI.[21] The fifth and last Member of the House to be expelled was Representative James A. Traficant, Jr., of Ohio, who was expelled on July 24, 2002, after his ten-count federal conviction for activities concerning the receipt of favors, gifts and money in return for performing official acts on behalf of the donors, and the receipt of salary kickbacks from staff.[22]

The numbers of actual expulsions from the House may be small because some Members of the House who have been found to have engaged in serious misconduct have chosen to resign (or have lost an election) before any formal action could be taken against them by the House. Thus, the House committees investigating allegations of misconduct have from time-to-time expressly recommended the expulsion of a Member, who then resigned before the expulsion vote could be taken by the full body.[23] Additionally, several other Members of the House who might have been subject to expulsion or other legislative discipline because of misconduct either resigned *before* any committee recommendation was made,[24] or, soon after their misconduct became known, lost their next election (either the primary or the general election) before congressional action was completed.[25] The defeat at the polls of Members who had engaged in misconduct was precisely the principal "ethics" oversight planned by the framers of the Constitution, who looked to the necessity of re-election to be the most efficient method of regulating Representatives' conduct. James Madison explained in the *Federalist Papers* that despite all the precautions taken by structural separation of powers in the government, or by the institution of the Congress or the law, the best control of Members' conduct would be their "habitual recollection of their dependence on the people" through the necessity "of frequent elections."[26]

Although the authority and power of each house of Congress to expel appears to be within the broad discretion of the institution, *policy* considerations, as opposed to questions of *power*, have generally restrained the House in exercising the authority to expel a Member when the conduct complained of occurred prior to the time the individual was elected to Congress,[27] or occurred in a prior Congress when the electorate knew of the conduct but still re-elected the Member. This restraint has been characterized in *dicta* by the Supreme Court as the House's "distrusting" its own "power" to expel for past misconduct.[28] While there has, in fact, in the past been some division of opinion on the subject of the House's constitutional "authority" or "right" to do so,[29] in modern congressional practice it would appear to be more accurate to say that such restraint has arisen from a questioning by the House of the wisdom of such a *policy*, rather than a formal recognition of an absence of constitutional *power* to expel for past misconduct.

The reticence of the House to expel a Member for past misconduct after the Member has been reelected by his or her constituents, with knowledge of the Member's conduct, appears to reflect the deference traditionally paid in our heritage to the popular will and election choice of the people.[30] Justice Story, while noting the necessity of expulsion of one who "disgrace[d] the house by the grossness of his conduct," noted that such power of the institution of the House to expel a duly-elected representative of the people is "at the same time so subversive of the rights of the people," as to require that it be used sparingly and to be "wisely guarded" by a two-thirds requirement.[31] Similarly, Cushing noted that the power to expel "should be governed by the strictest justice," since in expelling a duly elected Member without just cause, "a power of control would thus be assumed by the representative body over the constituent, wholly inconsistent with the freedom of election."[32]

The distinction between the "power" of the House to expel, and the judicious use of that power as a "policy" of the House, was cogently explained in a House Judiciary Committee report in 1914:

> In the judgment of your committee, the power of the House to expel or punish by censure a Member for misconduct occurring before his election or in a preceding or former Congress is sustained by the practice of the House, sanctioned by reason and sound policy and in extreme cases is absolutely essential to enable the House to exclude from its deliberations and councils notoriously corrupt men, who have unexpectedly and suddenly dishonored themselves and betrayed the public by acts and conduct rendering them unworthy of the high position of honor and trust reposed in them. ...
>
> But in considering this question and in arriving at the conclusions we have reached, we would not have you unmindful of the fact that we have been dealing with the question merely as one of *power*, and it should not be confused with the question of *policy* also involved. As a matter of sound policy, this extraordinary prerogative of the House, in our judgment, should be exercised only in extreme cases and always with great caution and after due circumspection, and should be invoked with greatest caution where the acts of misconduct complained of had become public previous to and were generally known at the time of the Member's election. To exercise such power in that instance the House might abuse its high prerogative, and in our opinion might exceed the just limitations of its constitutional authority by seeking to substitute its standards and ideals for the standards and ideals of the constituency of the member who had deliberately chosen him to be their Representative. The effect of such a policy would tend not to preserve but to undermine and destroy representative government.[33]

The power to expel is thus used cautiously when the institution of Congress might be seen as usurping or supplanting its own institutional judgment for the judgment of the electorate as to the character or fitness for office of an individual whom the people have chosen to represent them in Congress.[34]

As noted, the principal manner of dealing with ethical improprieties or misconduct of a Representative was intended by the Framers to be, and has historically been, reliance upon the voters to keep their Members "virtuous" through the "restraint of frequent elections."[35]

Consequences of Expulsion

Expulsion from the House of Representatives carries with it no further "automatic" penalties or disabilities beyond removal from Congress. Although the constitutions of some states provide that members expelled from their state legislatures are ineligible to be re-elected to that legislature, no such disability was included in the United States Constitution for Members of Congress. An individual who has been expelled from Congress is *not* ineligible to run again for that seat, or for another position in Congress. The three qualifications for congressional office—age, citizenship, and inhabitancy in the state—are established and fixed in the United States Constitution; are the *exclusive* qualifications to congressional office; and may not be added to or altered by Congress via a statute or internal congressional rule, or by a state unilaterally.[36] A Member who has been expelled from Congress and subsequently re-elected may, therefore, not be "excluded" from being seated in Congress based merely on the past misconduct and subsequent congressional discipline.[37] Although in theory, a previously expelled Member re-elected to Congress could, after having been seated, be expelled by a two-thirds vote for misconduct, even past misconduct, both the House and the Senate have not, as discussed above, as a practice expelled a Member for past misconduct when the electorate knew of the conduct and still elected or re-elected the Member.

A Member who has been expelled from the House does not lose his or her federal government pension automatically by virtue of the expulsion. Rather, federal government pensions earned, vested, or accumulated by officers and employees, including Members of Congress, are forfeited under the so-called "Hiss Act" upon the conviction of certain federal offenses that relate to espionage, treason, or other specific national security offenses. [38] Additionally, Members of Congress convicted of any one of a number of criminal offenses relating to public corruption will lose credit for all of their years of congressional service that would have otherwise accrued toward a federal pension.[39]

Procedure

The Supreme Court has also recognized a very broad discretion and authority in each house of Congress to discipline its Members under its own chosen *procedural* standards, generally without an established right to judicial review. The act of disciplining Members is carried out through the rulemaking authority of the House. The Supreme Court in describing the congressional disciplinary process in *United States v. Brewster*, has noted in *dicta*:

> The process of disciplining a Member in the Congress ... is not surrounded with the panoply of protective shields that are present in a criminal case. An accused Member is judged by no specifically articulated standards, and is at the mercy of an almost unbridled discretion of the charging body ... from whose decision there is no established right of review.[40]

Currently in the House of Representatives, a resolution to expel a Member would usually be referred to the House Committee on Ethics, the standing committee in the House with jurisdiction over congressional conduct and ethics, although such a resolution is considered to raise a question of the "privileges" of the House, and could be called up as a privileged resolution with notice by its sponsor according to House Rules.[41] The House Committee on Ethics is also authorized to receive "complaints" concerning a Member's conduct from any other Member of the House (or from outside of the House when certified by a Member),[42] may initiate on its own accord an investigation of a Member,[43] and may also be instructed by a resolution adopted by the House of Representatives to investigate a particular matter or Member. Under House Rule changes adopted in 2008, the House established an independent Office of Congressional Ethics for the House of Representatives, made up of non-Members of the House, which may initiate inquiries into allegations of misconduct by Members and staff, and may then refer matters to the standing House Committee on Ethics for further investigation and disciplinary recommendations.[44]

While it was a common practice in the past to wait until all appeals were exhausted in a criminal conviction of a Member before the House would proceed on a matter concerning that Member,[45] the more modern practice is for the House to take cognizance of the underlying *factual* findings regarding the conduct that was the basis for the Member's conviction, regardless of the potential *legal* or procedural issues which might be resolved on appeal.[46] The rules of the House Committee on Ethics specifically provide, in fact, for automatic jurisdiction of the committee when a Member has been convicted in a federal, state, or local court of a felony.[47] Moreover, in one instance, a committee disciplinary proceeding concerning a Member who had been indicted for bribery was begun after the Member's trial, even though the trial ended in a hung jury, and before a second trial was to commence.[48]

The current Rules of the House of Representatives authorize the House Committee on Ethics to investigate allegations of violations of "any law, rule, regulation, or other standard of conduct applicable to the conduct of such Member ... in the performance of his duties or the discharge of his responsibilities," and after such investigation the committee is to "report to the House its finding of fact and recommendations, if any...."[49] The committee has promulgated detailed procedural rules to implement fairness in the disciplinary process, specifically providing the requirements of notice, the specification of charges, and opportunities for the charged Member to be heard and to examine witnesses and evidence. After proceedings by an investigatory subcommittee, the taking of evidence and an adjudicatory hearing, if the Member is found by the majority of the committee members to have committed the specific offenses charged, the full committee will then consider the appropriate discipline.[50] If the committee finds that expulsion is warranted, a recommendation for such discipline is made in a report to the full House of Representatives, which may be, after debate, accepted, modified, or rejected by the House.

CENSURE

The term "censure," unlike the term "expel," does not appear in the Constitution, although the authority is derived from the same clause – Article I, Section 5, clause 2, concerning the authority of each house of Congress to "punish its Members for disorderly Behaviour." Censure, reprimand, or admonition are traditional ways in which parliamentary bodies have disciplined their members and maintained order and dignity in their proceedings.[51] In the House of Representatives, a "censure" is a formal vote by the majority of Members present and voting on a resolution disapproving a Member's conduct, generally with the additional requirement that the Member stand at the "well" of the House chamber to receive a verbal rebuke and reading of the censure resolution by the Speaker of the House.

Grounds

The Constitution, in providing that either house of Congress may "expel" a Member by a two-thirds majority, does not specify the reasons for such expulsion, but does in that same provision state that either house of Congress may punish its Members for "disorderly Behaviour." Some early commentators believed that the authority to "punish" a Member by way of censure or some other condemnation was thus expressly limited, unlike expulsion, to cases concerning "disorderly" or unruly behavior or conduct in Congress, that is, conduct which disrupts the institution.[52] The authority to discipline by way of censure, reprimand, or other such rebuke, however, has come to be recognized and accepted in congressional practice as extending to cases of "misconduct," even outside of Congress, which the House finds to be reprehensible, and/or to reflect discredit on the institution, and therefore, worthy of condemnation or rebuke.

The House of Representatives has taken a broad view of its authority to discipline its Members. In the 63rd Congress, for example, the House Judiciary Committee described the power of the House to punish for disorderly behavior as a power which is "full and plenary and may be enforced by summary proceedings. It is discretionary in character ... restricted by no limitation except in case of expulsion the requirement of the concurrence of a two-thirds vote."[53] Similarly, in its report on a Member, a House Select Committee in 1967 stated:

> Censure of a Member has been deemed appropriate in cases of a breach of the privileges of the House. There are two classes of privilege, the one, affecting the rights of the House collectively, its safety, dignity, and the integrity of its proceedings; and the other, affecting the rights, reputation, and conduct of Members, individually.
>
> Most cases of censure have involved the use of unparliamentary language, assaults upon a Member or insults to the House by introductions of offensive resolutions, but in five cases in the House and one in the Senate [as of 1967] censure was based on corrupt acts by a Member, and in another Senate case censure was based upon noncooperation with and abuse of Senate committees.
>
> * * *
>
> This discretionary power to punish for disorderly behavior is vested by the Constitution in the House of Representatives and its exercise is appropriate where a Member has been guilty of misconduct relating to his official duties, noncooperation with committees of this House, or nonofficial acts of a kind likely to bring this House into disrepute.[54]

Although the House has stated and demonstrated in precedents its reticence to *expel* a Member for misconduct in a previous Congress which was known to the electorate, the House has had no similar compunction nor has it exercised similar restraint in expressing a formal "censure" of such past misconduct. Thus, a House Select Committee in the 90th Congress noted that "the right to *censure* a Member for such prior acts is supported by clear precedent in both Houses of Congress.... "[55] In more recent years the House has adopted in its Rules a "statute of limitations" on actions, restricting the Ethics Committee from investigating alleged violations of conduct standards when such violations go back more than the last three Congresses, "unless the Committee determines that the alleged violation is directly related to an alleged violation that occurred in a more recent Congress."[56]

Precedents

In the House of Representatives, there have been 23 "censures" of Members (22 Members and 1 Delegate), including two censures of *former* Members who, in 1870, had resigned just prior to the House's consideration of expulsion motions against those Members for selling military academy appointments.[57] While the majority of the censures in the House occurred in the 19th century and concerned issues of decorum, that is, the use of unparliamentary or insulting language on the floor of the House or acts of violence towards other Members, in more recent years instances of financial misconduct appear to have been a major issue.[58] House Members have been censured for various conduct, including insulting or other unparliamentary language on the floor; assaulting another Member; supporting recognition of the Confederacy; the selling of military academy appointments; bribery; and in more recent years, for payroll fraud where inflated staff salaries were used to pay a Member's personal expenses;[59] receipt of improper gifts and improper use of campaign funds;[60] sexual misconduct with House pages;[61] and financial improprieties regarding the use of official letterhead to solicit private donations, impermissible use of rent-controlled facilities for one's campaign, and failure to file accurate financial disclosure reports and federal tax returns.[62]

Consequences of Censure

There is no specific disqualification or express consequence provided in the House Rules after a Member has been "censured." The political ignominy of being formally and publicly admonished and deprecated by one's colleagues, however, has led some Members of Congress who face a potential censure or other formal House discipline for certain misconduct to resign before any official recommendation or other action is taken.[63]

While there are no House Rules regarding the consequences of a "censure," the two political parties in the House themselves have adopted their own internal party rules which, in recent years, have generally barred from certain leadership positions, including the chairmanship of committees and subcommittees, those Members who have been censured during that Congress. Political party rules of the parties in the House may be changed by the particular party caucus or conference itself according to its own rules.

Reprimand

Prior to the 1970s in the House of Representatives, although there were some inconsistencies,[64] the terms "reprimand" and "censure" were often considered synonymous and used together in a resolution. In 1921, for example, a resolution adopted by the House instructed the Speaker to summon Representative Blanton of Texas "to the bar of the House and deliver to him its reprimand and censure."[65]

The more formalized distinction in the House whereby it is considered that a "reprimand" expressly involves a lesser level of disapproval of the conduct of a Member than that of a "censure," and is thus a less severe rebuke by the institution,[66] is of relatively recent origin. The term "reprimand" was used to explicitly indicate a less severe rebuke by the House in 1976 in the reprimand of a Member for his failure to disclose certain personal interests in official matters, and for the apparent use of his office to further his own personal financial interests.[67] Procedurally in the House, a "censure" resolution will generally involve a verbal admonition, such as a reading of the resolution, to be administered by the Speaker of the House to the Member at the bar of the House. In the case of a "reprimand," however, the resolution is merely adopted by a vote of the House with the Member "standing in his place," or is merely implemented by the adoption of the committee's report.[68]

Ten House Members have been "reprimanded" by the full House for a range of misconduct, including failure to disclose certain personal interests in official matters and using one's office to further one's personal gains; misrepresentations to investigating committees; failure to report campaign contributions; conversion of campaign contributions to personal use and false statements before the investigating committee; false statements on financial disclosure forms; ghost voting and maintaining persons on the official payroll not performing official duties commensurate with pay; the misuse of one's political influence in administrative matters to help a personal associate; the failure to insure that a Member-affiliated tax-exempt organization was not improperly involved in partisan politics, and for providing inaccurate, incomplete and unreliable information to the investigating committee; and the misuse of official resources by compelling congressional staff to work on political campaigns.[69] In 2009, the House of Representatives adopted a resolution of disapproval (and which thus would be considered to be a "reprimand" by the entire body of the House), stating that the House "disapproves" of the behavior of a Member "interrupting" the President's remarks to the House and Senate, which the House found to be "a breach of decorum" that "degraded the proceedings of the joint session."[70]

When the House Committee on Ethics makes a report recommending to the House a "censure" or a "reprimand," it may also include in that report a recommendation for an additional action such as a fine, a restitution or payment of funds, or recommendations for the loss of seniority or privileges, when such actions are deemed appropriate.

FINES; MONETARY ASSESSMENTS

In addition to more traditional disciplines of censure, reprimand, or expulsion, the House of Representatives as an institution has the authority to levy a fine against a Member of the House concerning a disciplinary matter. This authority appears to be incidental to the express constitutional grant of power to the House to determine the rules of its proceedings and to punish its Members for misconduct. *Deschler's Precedents* states expressly that under the constitutional authority of the House at Article I, Section 5, clause 2: "A fine may be levied by the House against a Member pursuant to its constitutional authority to punish its Members."[71] The House Committee on Ethics notes expressly in its Committee Rules that sanctions that it may recommend to the House concerning a Member may include expulsion, censure, reprimand, denial or limitation of any right, privilege or immunity of the Member, or a "fine."[72] The authority for each house of Congress to fine one of its own Members was recognized by the Supreme Court in *dicta* in *Kilbourn v. Thompson*,[73] where the Court noted that "either House" of Congress has "the power of punishment ... by fine or imprisonment," relating to areas where Congress has been expressly granted authority, such as where the "Constitution expressly empowers each House to punish its own Members for disorderly behavior."[74]

Fines for disciplinary purposes in the House, as well as in the Senate,[75] have been relatively infrequent occurrences.[76] The precedents in the House have demonstrated that the House fined a Member in 1969 the sum of $25,000 to be repaid by automatically withdrawing a certain amount regularly from his pay, for various conduct offenses, including the misuse of official committee appropriations, payroll, and expenses.[77] A Member of the House who was censured in 1979 was required to "make restitution of substantial amounts by which he was unjustly enriched," that is, the Member was expressly ordered within the resolution of censure to pay to the House a specific amount by executing an interest-bearing demand promissory note for $40,031.66, made payable to the Treasury of the United States.[78] A Member of the House who was officially "reprimanded" by the House in 2012 for misuse of official resources in compelling official congressional staff to work on political campaigns was also "fined" $10,000 as part of the reprimand.[79]

At other times the House pursuant to disciplinary actions required certain monetary assessments of Members of Congress which were not expressly or necessarily characterized as "fines." A Member of Congress, pursuant to a formal "reprimand" was required to make restitution to the District of Columbia of certain monies and fines, concerning which he had improperly used his influence to have "fixed" or reduced.[80] In 1997, a monetary assessment or penalty, which was not characterized by the committee as a "fine," was imposed upon the Speaker of the House to pay "for some of the costs" of an ethics investigation which resulted in the reprimand of the Speaker.[81]

The "fines" and/or monetary assessments ordered in the disciplinary cases appear to involve the repayment or restitution of funds misused or wrongfully received, as opposed to fines merely or strictly for "punishment" purposes and not necessarily connected to the wrongful conduct. This is consistent with the current guidance in the House Committee on Ethics Rules concerning the recommendation of a "fine," which the committee notes, "is appropriate in a case in which it is likely that the violation was committed to secure a personal financial benefit."[82] There does not appear to be, however, a constitutional or institutional *requirement* for such fines to be so connected with unjust enrichments or misuse of funds; and the Committee on Ethics has noted in its Rules that the guidance concerning fines and other sanctions recommended to the House "sets forth general guidelines and does not limit the authority of the Committee to recommend other sanctions."[83]

Suspension

Although a temporary "suspension" is traditionally listed as one of the possible disciplinary actions that a legislative body may take against one of its members,[84] the House of Representatives has in recent years questioned its authority to disqualify or mandatorily suspend a Member by a simple majority vote.[85] Such a "suspension" would most likely involve a prohibition on a Member of the House from voting on or working on legislative or representational matters for a particular time. Although not addressing a "suspension" specifically, the House has generally considered a decision of a Member not to vote on a matter as within the discretionary purview of the Member individually under House Rule III(1), even when a legislative matter may involve possible conflicting personal interests. As noted by the House, its authority to require a Member to disqualify himself or herself from voting has traditionally been questioned, and such "recusal" has therefore been traditionally left to the discretion of the Member. *Jefferson's Manual and Rules of the House of Representatives*, at §658, states:

> [T]he weight of authority also favors the idea that there is no authority in the House to deprive a Member of the right to vote (V, 5937, 5952, 5959, 5966, 5967; VIII, 3072). In one or two early instances the Speaker has decided that because of a personal interest, a Member should not vote (V, 5955, 5958); but on all other occasions and in the later practice the Speaker has held that the Member himself and not the Chair should determine this question (V, 5950, 5951; VIII, 3071; Speaker Albert, Dec. 2, 1975, p. 38135; Speaker O'Neill, Mar. 1, 1979, p. 3748), and the Speaker has denied his own power to deprive a Member of the constitutional right to vote (V, 5956; Speaker Albert, Dec. 2, 1975, p. 38135; Speaker O'Neill, Mar. 1, 1979, p. 3748).[86]

As to refraining from voting and committee work specifically, the House of Representatives in the 94th Congress adopted a rule which stated a sense of the House that Members who have been convicted of a crime for which a sentence of two or more years may be imposed "should refrain from participation in the business of each committee of which he is then a member and should refrain from voting on any question at a meeting of the House, or of the Committee of the Whole House ..." until there has been a judicial or administrative reinstatement of his or her presumption of innocence, or until the Member is re-elected.[87] The supporters of the provision noted that the rule was worded in a *discretionary* manner because, they believed, that if the provisions were mandatory, then "it would have been unconstitutional [because] [i]t would have deprived the district, which the Member was elected to represent, of representation.... "[88]

Although the Rule on refraining from voting is couched in what can be considered advisory terms of guidance to Members, the Rules of the House also provide, in the Code of Official Conduct, that Members of the House "shall adhere to the spirit and the letter of the Rules of the House."[89] Members are thus expected to conform to and abide by the abstention provision.[90]

Letters of Reproval and Other Committee Actions

In the House of Representatives, a "Letter of Reproval" is an administrative action of the House Committee on Ethics, authorized under the Rules of the House of Representatives "to establish or enforce standards of official conduct for members, officers, and employees of the House."[91] The issuance of a Letter of Reproval by the committee is made public, as it is issued as part of a public report from the committee to the House on an "investigation" that the House Committee on Ethics has undertaken.[92]

A Letter of Reproval may be sent by the Committee on Ethics on its own accord by majority vote of the committee, without any approval or action by the full House of Representatives.[93] As such, a Letter of Reproval is clearly distinguishable from legislative "discipline," "punishment," or "sanctions" that the full House may invoke against a Member, such as censure, reprimand, fine, or expulsion.[94] It appears that a Letter of Reproval is intended to be an action by the committee which is an alternative to the recommendation of sanctions to the House, and is an action which is used for infractions of Rules or standards which, because of the nature of the infractions or because of mitigating circumstances, do not rise to the level of requiring action by the full House of Representatives. The Rules of the Committee on Ethics provide, after setting out procedures when "a majority of the Committee does not vote in favor of the recommendation that the House of Representatives take action," that "[T]he Committee may also, by majority vote, adopt a motion to issue a Letter of Reproval or take other appropriate Committee action."[95] The committee may issue such Letter "[i]f the Committee determines a Letter of Reproval constitutes sufficient action.... "[96] The committee procedural rules appear to indicate that such a "Letter of Reproval" may be sent only after an investigatory subcommittee has issued a Statement of Alleged Violations, at least one count of which has been proved by an adjudicatory subcommittee, and upon completion of a sanction hearing.[97]

A Letter of Reproval was characterized by the ethics committee in the House—then known as the House Committee on Standards of Official Conduct—as a "rebuke of a Member's conduct issued by a body of that Member's peers acting, as the Committee on Standards of Official Conduct, on behalf of the House of Representatives."[98] The House Ethics Committee has issued Letters of Reproval for the improper use of campaign accounts for personal loans;[99] for a Member's borrowing of campaign funds for personal use, and a subsequent "inadequate" disclosure of such transaction;[100] and concerning allegations of sexual harassment of a female employee, and the use of one's office for political campaign activity.[101] In October of 2000, after a lengthy investigation of a Member, the committee issued a Letter of Reproval for actions for which the Member was found to have "brought discredit to the House of Representatives," including a relationship with a former chief of staff which gave the appearance that official decisions might have been improperly affected, violations of the House gift rule, misuse of official congressional resources, misuse of official congressional staff for campaign purposes, and the appearance that certain expenditures of the Member's campaign committee were not for bona fide campaign or political purposes.[102] In June of 2001, the committee issued a Letter of Reproval to a Member for the improper expenditure of campaign funds to benefit businesses in which the Member and his family had a personal stake, and for the improper conversion of campaign funds to personal uses.[103]

In addition to a formal, public "Letter of Reproval," the committee has addressed ethical issues concerning allegations of misconduct by Members by way of "other appropriate Committee action," upon agreement of a majority of the committee, when an investigation is undertaken by a subcommittee but the recommendation of sanctions to the full House is not made.[104] Such actions by the full committee have included writing a letter to a Member concerning "necessary corrective action" that should be taken by the Member, or by noting "poor judgment" and the creation of an "appearance of impropriety."[105] The committee has also noted violations of House Rules or standards, has "so notified" the Member, and announced that no further action by the committee will be taken.[106] In 1990, the committee made a public report concerning a Member's behavior, noting that the "Committee clearly disapproves" of the Member's conduct.[107] In 2004, after an investigation by an investigatory subcommittee, the full committee issued a report which "will serve as a public admonishment by the Committee" of three Members.[108] Similarly, in 2006, the committee made public a report from its investigative subcommittee finding that a Member's actions with regard to the release of recordings of intercepted telephone conversations of other Members "were not consistent with the spirit of the Committee's rules."[109] The committee issued "a public admonishment" of a Member in 2010 for accepting gifts of travel in violation of the House gifts rule, and required the Member to "repay the costs of the trips to the respective entities that paid for his travel."[110] In 2012, the Ethics Committee reported that it "agrees with the findings and conclusions of the Investigative Subcommittee" concerning a violation of House Rules by a Member "improperly using her official position for her beneficial interest by permitting her office to take official action specifically on behalf of her husband's medical practice."[111] Specifically, the report from the investigative subcommittee "recommends that the Committee issue this Report, and that this Report serve as a reproval" of the Member.[112]

The Ethics Committee in the House has characterized past actions such as these generally by stating that the committee "has publicly admonished several other Members for their conduct."[113] Such informal notifications, public reports, public admonishments, or letters for corrective action, thus may be distinguished from those instances when the committee "formally and publicly reproved" a Member by way of a formal "Letter of Reproval,"[114] although it may be argued that these other committee actions are to some degree comparable since they are all "administrative action[s]" taken by the committee itself "pursuant to an investigation" that had been conducted by an investigative subcommittee of the Committee on Ethics.[115]

The committee has also sent a so-called "letter of admonition" to a Member against whom a complaint was filed by another Member of the House,[116] which was apparently different from, and was not technically, a "Letter of Reproval" or even any other "administrative" action "pursuant to an investigation" by an investigatory subcommittee of the committee.[117] The "letter of admonition" in this case was a method of disposing of a complaint by the committee upon the recommendation of the Chairman and Ranking Minority Member of the committee for a "resolution of the complaint by a letter to the Member ... against whom the complaint is made,"[118] without moving forward with a subcommittee investigation.

APPENDIX. DISCIPLINARY ACTIONS TAKEN BY THE FULL HOUSE AGAINST A MEMBER

Table A-1. Censure

Date	Member of Congress	Conduct
1. July 11, 1832	William Stanberry (Ohio)	Insulting the Speaker of the House.
2. Mar. 22, 1842	Joshua R. Giddings (Ohio)	Resolution introduced by Member relating to delicate international negotiations deemed "incendiary."
3. July 15, 1856	Lawrence M. Keitt (S.C.)	Assisting in assault on a Member.
4. April 9, 1864	Benjamin G. Harris (Md.)	Treasonous conduct in opposing subjugation of the South.
5. April 14, 1864	Alexander Long (Ohio)	Supporting recognition of the Confederacy.
6. May 14, 1866	John W. Chanler (N.Y.)	Insulting the House by introduction of resolution containing unparliamentary language.
7. July 24, 1866	Lovell H. Rousseau (Ky.)	Assault of another Member.
8. Jan. 26, 1867	John W. Hunter (N.Y.)	Unparliamentary language.
9. Jan. 15, 1868	Fernando Wood (N.Y.)	Unparliamentary language.
10. Feb. 14, 1869	Edward D. Holbrook (Idaho)	Unparliamentary language.
11. Feb. 24, 1870	Benjamin Whittemore (S.C.)	Selling military academy appointments (Member had resigned before expulsion, and was "condemned" by House).
12. Mar. 1, 1870	John T. DeWeese (S.C.)	Selling military academy appointments (Member had resigned before expulsion, and was "condemned" by House).
13. Mar. 16, 1870	Roderick R. Butler (Tenn.)	Accepting money for "political purposes" in return for Academy appointment.
14. Feb. 27, 1873	Oakes Ames (Mass.)	Bribery in "Credit Mobilier" case. (Conduct prior to election to House.)
15. Feb. 27, 1873	James Brooks (N.Y.)	Bribery in "Credit Mobilier" case. (Conduct prior to election to House.)
16. Feb. 4, 1875	John Y. Brown (Ky.)	Unparliamentary language.
17. May 17, 1890	William D. Bynum (Ind.)	Unparliamentary language.
18. Oct. 27, 1921	Thomas L. Blanton (Tex.)	Unparliamentary language.

Table A-1. (Continued)

Date	Member of Congress	Conduct
19. July 31, 1979	Charles C. Diggs (Mich.)	Payroll fraud, 18 U.S.C. §1001 conviction.
20. June 6, 1980	Charles H. Wilson (Cal.)	Receipt of improper gifts; "ghost" employees; improper personal use of campaign funds.
21. July 20, 1983	Gerry E. Studds (Mass.)	Sexual misconduct with House page.
22. July 20, 1983	Daniel B. Crane (Ill.)	Sexual misconduct with House page.
23. Dec. 2, 2010	Charles B. Rangel (N.Y.)	Misuse of congressional letterhead for fundraising; impermissible use of rent-controlled facility for campaign headquarters; inaccurate financial disclosure reports and federal tax returns.

Table A-2. Reprimand

Date	Member of Congress	Conduct
1. July 29, 1976	Robert L.F. Sikes (Fla.)	Use of office for personal gain; failure to disclose interest in legislation.
2. Oct. 13, 1978	Charles H. Wilson (Cal.)	False statement before Standards of Official Conduct Committee investigating Korean influence matter.
3. Oct. 13, 1978	John J. McFall (Cal.)	Failure to report campaign contributions from Korean lobbyist.
4. Oct. 13, 1978	Edward J. Roybal (Cal.)	Failure to report campaign contributions; false sworn statement before Standards of Official Conduct Committee investigating Korean influence matter.
5. July 31, 1984	George V. Hansen (Idaho)	False statements on financial disclosure form; conviction under 18 U.S.C. §1001 for such false statements.
6. Dec. 18, 1987	Austin J. Murphy (Pa.)	Ghost voting (allowing another person to cast his vote); maintaining on his payroll persons not performing official duties commensurate with pay.
7. July 26, 1990	Barney Frank (Mass.)	Using political influence to fix parking tickets and influence probation officers for personal friend.
8. Jan. 21, 1997	Newt Gingrich (Ga.)	Allowing a Member-affiliated tax-exempt organization to be used for political purposes; providing inaccurate and unreliable information to the ethics committee.

Date	Member of Congress	Conduct
9. Sept. 15, 2009	Joe Wilson (S.C.)	Interrupting the President's remarks to a joint session of the House and Senate which was found to be a "breach of decorum
		and degraded the proceedings of the joint session."
10. Aug. 2, 2012	Laura Richardson (Calif.)	Compelling official congressional staff to work on political campaign.

Table A-3. Expulsion

Date	Member of Congress	Conduct
1. July 13, 1861	John B. Clark (Mo.)	Disloyalty to the Union - taking up arms against the United States.
2. Dec. 2, 1861	John W. Reid (Mo.)	Disloyalty to the Union - taking up arms against the United States.
3. Dec. 3, 1861	Henry C. Burnett (Ky.)	Disloyalty to the Union - taking up arms against the United States.
4. Oct. 2, 1980	Michael J. Myers (Pa.)	Bribery conviction for accepting money in return for promise to use influence in immigration matters.
5. July 24, 2002	James A. Traficant (Ohio)	Conviction of conspiracy to commit bribery and to defraud U.S., receipt of illegal gratuities, obstruction of justice, filing false tax returns, and racketeering, in connection with receipt of favors and money in return for official acts; and receipt of salary kickbacks from staff.

Source: Congressional Research Service files; House Committee on Standards of Official Conduct, "Historical Summary of Conduct Cases in the House of Representatives" (November 2004).

End Notes

[1] Deschler's precedents of the united states house of representatives, h. Doc. 94-661, 94th cong., 2d sess., volume 3, ch. 12, § 12, p. 168 (1979); Justice Joseph Story, Commentaries on the constitution of the united states, vol. Ii, § 835 (boston 1883).

[2] Cushing, The law and practice of legislative assemblies, pp.250-251, 257-259, 268-270 (Boston 1874). Internal disciplinary action is "rooted in the judgment of the House as to what was necessary or appropriate for it to do to assure the integrity of its legislative performance and its institutional acceptability to the people at large as a serious and responsible instrument of government." Deschler's Precedents, supra at 174, citing Powell v. McCormack, 395 F.2d

577, McGowan concurring, at 607 (D.C.Cir. 1968), rev'd on other grounds, 395 U.S. 486 (1969); Story, supra at § 835. Note British Parliamentary practice: "The practice of expulsion is not so much disciplinary as remedial, not so much to punish Members as to rid the House of persons who are unfit for membership." Erskine may, law, privileges, proceedings and usage of parliament, at 105 (London 1964).

[3] House ethics action does not foreclose a criminal prosecution on the same matter. United States v. Rose, 28 F.3d 181, 189-190 (D.C.Cir. 1994); 2 Op. Atty. Gen. 655 (1834); United States v. Traficant, 368 F.3d 646 (6th Cir. 2004), cert. denied, 543 U.S. 1055 (2005).

[4] Under the "Speech or Debate" clause of the Constitution (Article I, Section 6, cl. 1), Members of Congress may not be questioned outside of Congress "for any Speech or Debate in either House," that is, they are immune from criminal or civil proceedings only for their official conduct or activities which are deemed to be "an integral part of the deliberative and communicative processes by which Members participate in committee and House proceedings." Gravel v. United States, 408 U.S. 606, 625 (1972). The constitutional bar to the "Arrest" of Members during their attendance of, or "going to and returning from" a session of Congress for other than a felony or "Breach of the Peace" (Article I, Section 6, cl. 1), is an "obsolete" provision which applies only to arrests in civil suits, common in the 18th century, but does not apply to criminal arrests. Williamson v. United States, 207 U.S. 425, 446 (1908); Long v. Ansell, 293 U.S. 76 (1934); Gravel, supra at 614; Deschler's precedents, supra at Ch. 12, § 3.1; see discussion in The Constitution Of The United States, Analysis And Interpretation, S. Doc. 103-6, 103rd Cong., 1st Sess., at 127 (1996). Contrary to popular myth and misunderstanding, Members of Congress are not constitutionally immune from arrest for traffic violations under this clause.

[5] Alexander Hamilton, Ii Eliot's Debates 257; note also James Madison, 2 Farrand, Records Of The Federal Convention Of 1787, 249-250, and The Federalist Papers, No. 57; Powell v. McCormack, 395 U.S. 486, 508, 509, 531 (1969).

[6] See footnote 2, supra; Story, supra at §§ 835-836. Note also Senator John Quincy Adams' arguments in 1807 on Senate's authority to expel a Member even after re-election, II Hinds' Precedents Of The House Of RepresentativeS, § 1264, p. 817 (1907).

[7] Rules of the House Committee on Ethics, Rule 24(e) (February 5, 2013, 113th Congress); Deschler's Precedents, supra at Ch. 12, § 12.

[8] House Committee on Ethics, Rule 24(g).

[9] In re Chapman, 166 U.S. 661, 669-670 (1897); H.Rept. 570, 63rd Cong., 2d Sess. (1914) (Judiciary Committee), at Vi Cannon's Precedents Of The House Of Representatives, § 398, p. 558; Brown, House Practice, Guide To The Rules, Precedents And Procedures Of The House, 104th Cong., 2d Sess. "Misconduct; Sanctions," at 581-582 (1996). Note authority of Committee on Ethics, Rules of the House of Representatives, Rule XI, para. 3(a)(2), and Code of Official Conduct, Rule XXIII(1).

[10] See the Appendix for a listing of House disciplinary actions.

[11] Brown, supra, "Voting," at p. 908: "A two-thirds vote ordinarily means two-thirds of those voting, a quorum being present, and not two-thirds of the entire membership."

[12] Powell v. McCormack, 395 U.S. 486, 522 (1969). Deschler's Precedents, supra at Ch. 12, §12, p. 169, n. 21.

[13] See case of Senator William Blount of Tennessee, expelled on July 8, 1797; and found not subject to impeachment. III Hinds' Precedents, supra at §§ 2294-2318.

[14] II HINDS' PRECEDENTS, supra at § 1275.

[15] Bowman and Bowman, Article I, Section 5: Congress' Power to Expel - An Exercise in Self Restraint, 29 Syracuse Law Review 1071, 1089-1090 (1978).

[16] Story, supra at § 836.

[17] II Hinds' Precedents, supra at §1263. See footnote 12, supra.

[18] 166 U.S. 661, 669-670 (1897).

[19] House Committee on Ethics, Rule 24(g).

[20] See House expulsions of Representative-elect John B. Clark of Missouri (1861), Representative John W. Reid of Missouri (1861), and Representative Henry C. Burnett of Kentucky (1861), for disloyalty to the Union. II Hinds' Precedents, supra at §§ 1261,1262.

[21] H.Rept. 96-1387 (1980), In the Matter of Representative Michael J. Myers, 126 CONG. REC. 28,978 (October 2, 1980). Representative Myers was expelled after conviction for bribery, conspiracy and violation of the Travel Act.

[22] H.Rept. 107-594 (2002), In the Matter of Representative James A. Traficant, Jr., 148 Cong. Rec. 14318-14319 (July 24, 2002). Representative Traficant was expelled after conviction of conspiracy to violate federal bribery laws, receipt of illegal gratuities, obstruction of justice, conspiracy to defraud the United States, filing false income tax returns, and racketeering.

[23] Note, e.g., H.Rept. 97-110 (1981), In the Matter of Representative Raymond F. Lederer, and House Committee on Standards recommendation of expulsion for bribery; and H.Rept. 100-506 (1988), In the Matter of Representative Mario Biaggi, recommendation of expulsion after conviction for illegal gratuities, Travel Act violations, and obstruction of justice. Note case of Rep. B.F. Whittemore, recommended for expulsion by Military Affairs Committee for sale of Military Academy appointments, who subsequently resigned in 1870, and who was then censured in absentia by the House (II Hinds' Precedents, supra at § 1273); and House censure of John DeWeese after his resignation (also for the sale of Academy appointments), but before the committee reported the resolution of expulsion. II Hinds' Precedents, supra at § 1239. See also expulsion resolutions, reported from an ad hoc committee, for bribery, and subsequent resignations during House consideration of resolutions, by Representatives William Gilbert, Frances Edwards, and Orasmus Matteson, in 1857 (II Hinds' Precedents, supra at § 1275).

[24] H.Rept. 96-1537, at 10-11 (1980), In the Matter of Representative John W. Jenrette, Jr.; H.Rept. 104-886, at 19 (1997), Summary of Activities, One Hundred Fourth Congress (concerning Representative Mel Reynolds); H.Rept. 101-995, at 10-11 (1990), Summary of Activities, One Hundred First Congress (concerning Representative Donald E. Lukens), and at 12-13 (concerning Representative Robert Garcia); H.Rept. 96-856, (1980), In the Matter of Representative Daniel J. Flood (1980); H.Rept. 109-744 (2007), Summary of Activities, One Hundred Ninth Congress (concerning Representative Robert Ney), and at 17-18 (concerning representative Tom DeLay). Representative Randy "Duke" Cunningham resigned from the House on December 1, 2005, after pleading guilty to a criminal conspiracy to commit bribery and tax evasion. Since no recommendations were made by the committee regarding these Members, it cannot be said with certainty what, if any, discipline would have been recommended by the committee, or approved by the House.

[25] The House Committee on Ethics (formerly the Committee on Standards of Official Conduct) has found that since it will "lose jurisdiction" over a Member who has been defeated in an election, proceedings which could not be completed prior to the January end-of-term be suspended. Note, for example, H.Rept. 110-938, at 18 (2009), Summary of Activities, One Hundred Tenth Congress (concerning Representative William Jefferson); H.Rept. 105-848, at 14 (1999), Summary of Activities, One Hundred Fifth Congress (concerning Representative Jay C. Kim); H.Rept. 104-886, supra at 21 (concerning Representative Barbara-Rose Collins); see also H.Rept. 100-1125, at 17 (1989), Summary of Activities,

One Hundredth Congress (concerning Rep. Patrick L. Swindall); H.Rept. 95-1818, at 3 (1978), Summary of Activities, Ninety-Fifth Congress (concerning Rep. Joshua Eilberg).

[26] Madison. The Federalist Papers, No. 57: "All these sanctions, however, would be found very insufficient without the restraint of frequent elections ... as to support in the members an habitual recollection of their dependence on the people."

[27] Deschler's Precedents, supra at Ch. 12, § 13, p. 176. See H.Rept. 94-1477, at 2 (1976), In the Matter of Representative Andrew J. Hinshaw, where the House Committee on Standards of Official Conduct recommended against expulsion of a Member, since the Member's conviction "while reflecting on his moral turpitude, does not relate to his official conduct while a Member of Congress."

[28] The Court in Powell v. McCormack, supra, in distinguishing the exclusion of Powell from an expulsion, noted that the House has "distrusted" its right to expel Members for prior conduct after they have been reelected (395 U.S. at 508), and that congressional precedents have shown that "the House will not expel a member for misconduct committed during an earlier Congress." 395 U.S. at 509, noting expulsion case of John W. Langley, H.Rept. 30, 69th Cong., 1st Sess., 1-2 (1925). The Court noted specifically, however, that it was not ruling on Congress' authority to expel for past misconduct (395 U.S. at 507, n. 27; 510, n.30), and, in fact, Justice Douglas, in his concurrence noted specifically that "if this were an expulsion case I would think that no justiciable controversy were presented" (395 U.S. at 553), since Douglas agreed with Senator Murdock of Utah in a 1940 exclusion case that each House may "expel anyone it designates by a two-thirds vote." 395 U.S. at 558-559.

[29] Note conflicting opinions of two House committees in the Credit Mobilier investigations on the discipline of Representatives Ames and Brooks in the 42nd Congress, H.Rept. 77, 42nd Cong., 3rd Sess. (1872) and H.Rept. 82, 42d Cong., 3rd Sess. (1872). The House specifically refused, however, to accept a preamble to the substitute resolution for censure expressly questioning its authority to expel for past misconduct. See Committee Print, House of Representatives Exclusion, Censure and Expulsion Cases from 1789 to 1973, 93rd Cong., 1st Sess. 125 (1973); note also majority and minority opinions in expulsion cases of William S. King and John Schumaker, H.Rept. 815, 44th Cong., 1st Sess. (1876), II Hinds' Precedents, supra at §1283, and in expulsion case of Orsamus B. Matteson, H.Rept. 179, 35th Cong., 1st Sess. (1858), II Hinds' Precedents § 1285.

[30] See footnote 5, supra. Note also discussion of the infamous Wilkes case in England, shortly before the time of the drafting of the United States Constitution. Powell v. McCormack, supra at 532-535; May, supra at 107.

[31] Story, supra at § 835.

[32] Cushing, supra at § 625; Deschler's Precedents, supra at Ch. 12, §13, p. 175.

[33] H.Rept. 570, 63rd Cong., 2d Sess. (1914), at VI Cannon's Precedents, supra at § 398. Emphasis added.

[34] "Congress has demonstrated a clear reluctance to expel when to do so would impinge ... on the electoral process." Bowman and Bowman, supra at 1101.

[35] Madison, The Federalist Papers, No. 57.

[36] Powell v. McCormack, supra; U.S. Term Limits, Inc. v. Thornton, 514 U.S. 779 (1995); Cook v. Gralike, 531 U.S. 510 (2001).

[37] See Powell v. McCormack, supra at 522, 547-550, 537 n. 69. Note discussion by the Court (at 527-536) of the Wilkes case concerning English parliamentary practice at the time of the Constitution's drafting. If, however, there is alleged disloyalty to the Union, after having taken an oath of office to defend the Constitution, the disqualification provision of the

Fourteenth Amendment may come into play. See pre-Powell, House of Representatives case of Victor Berger, excluded even after re-election. VI Cannon's Precedents, §§ 56, 58, 59.

[38] See now 5 U.S.C. § 8311 et seq. The President is not covered by the retirement laws applicable to other officers and employees of the federal government, and forfeiture of retired pay applies in case of impeachment, conviction, and removal of the President. See P.L. 85-745, as amended, 3 U.S.C. § 102, note.

[39] P.L. 110-81, the "Honest Leadership and Open Government Act," Sections 401(a) and 401(b), and P.L. 112-105, the "STOCK Act," Section 15, amending 5 U.S.C. § 8332 (CSRS) and 5 U.S.C. § 8411 (FERS).

[40] 408 U.S. 501, 519 (1972). Matters "textually committed" to Congress in the Constitution, such as rules for internal proceedings, might not generally be subject to judicial review unless another, express provision of the Constitution is violated. Note, e.g., Nixon v. United States, 506 U.S. 224, 228-229, 236-238 (1993); United States v. Ballin, 144 U.S. 1, 5 (1892); Powell v. McCormack, supra at 519, and 553 (Douglas, J. concurring).

[41] House Rule IX. Deschler's Precedents, supra, Ch. 12, § 13, at 176-177; Brown, supra, "Misconduct," § 21. Note also H.Rept. 94-1477, at 6 (1976), In the Matter of Representative Andrew J. Hinshaw. Prior to 1968 when the standing ethics committee, then called the Committee on Standards of Official Conduct, was created, such resolutions were referred to either ad hoc select committees, or to standing committees with other jurisdiction, such as Judiciary.

[42] House Rule XI, para. 3(b)(2).

[43] House Rule XI, para. 3(b)(2); House Committee on Ethics, Rules 14(a)(3), 15.

[44] H.Res. 895, 110th Congress. See CRS Report R40760, House Office of Congressional Ethics: History, Authority, and Procedures, by Jacob R. Straus.

[45] Deschler's Precedents, supra, Ch. 12, § 13, at 176.

[46] Note discussion in H.Rept. 96-1387, supra at 4-5; see also, generally, CRS Rpt. 88-197A, "House Discipline of Members After Conviction But Before Final Appeal," March 1, 1988 (archived). A Member convicted of a felony for which the penalty may be two years or more imprisonment, "should refrain" from voting on the floor or in committee until his or her presumption of innocence is restored. House Rule XXIII (10).

[47] House Committee on Ethics, Rule 14(a)(4), 18(e).

[48] H.Rept. 96-856 (1980), In the Matter of Representative Daniel J. Flood (1980).

[49] House Rule XI, cl. 3(a)(2).

[50] Investigations subcommittees are four Members of the House, and may be made up of committee Members, as well as Members of the House not on the committee who are appointed at the beginning of the Congress as a reserve "pool" available to be on investigations subcommittees if needed. Adjudications are held before a panel of the committee who did not serve on the investigations subcommittee, and if any charges drafted by the investigations subcommittee are proven before the adjudications panel, a "sanctions" hearing to determine the sanctions to be recommended to the House is conducted before the full membership of the Ethics Committee. House Rule X, cl. 5(a)(3) and (4), XI, cl. 3(b)(1)(B)(i), Rules of the Committee on Ethics, supra.

[51] May, The Law, Privileges, Proceedings And Usage Of Parliament, supra at 103; BLACK'S LAW DICTIONARY, at 224, 6th Edition (1990), defines "censure" as: "The formal resolution of a legislative, administrative, or other body reprimanding a person, normally one of its own members, for specified conduct."

[52] Note, for example, discussion in Bowman and Bowman, supra at 1089 - 1091, citing Rawle, View Of The Constitution Of United States 46-47 (2nd ed. 1829).

[53] H.Rept. 570, 63rd Cong., 2d Sess. (1914).

[54] H.Rept. 27, 90th Cong., 1st Sess., at 24-26, 29 (1967), In re Adam Clayton Powell. The Select Committee recommended to the full House in the 90th Congress to seat Mr. Powell, and then to censure him. The House rejected that recommendation, however, and voted to "exclude" Powell, which was ultimately found unconstitutional by the Supreme Court in Powell v. McCormack, supra, because the House's exclusion action went beyond judging the three constitutional "qualifications" or the "election" of the Member-elect. Representative Powell was re-elected to and then seated in the 91st Congress, but was fined and had his seniority reduced by the House (H.Res. 2, 115 Cong. Rec. 29, 34 (January 3, 1969)).

[55] H.Rept. 27, supra at 27; see also censure of Representatives Ames and Brooks in the "Credit Mobilier" bribery matter (1872), for conduct that took place at least five years before their election to the House, and about which the electorate apparently knew, II Hinds' Precedents, supra at § 1286; DESCHLER'S PRECEDENTS, supra at Ch. 12, §16, pp. 194-195; and H.Rept. 96-351, at 3-5 (1979), In the Matter of Representative Charles C. Diggs, Jr.

[56] House Rule XI, cl. 3(b)(3).

[57] See censures of Representatives Whittemore and DeWeese, Ii Hinds' Precedents, supra at §§ 1273, 1239.

[58] See Appendix; also, House Committee on Standards of Official Conduct, "Historical Summary of Conduct Cases in the House of Representatives" (November 2004); House of Representatives Exclusion, Censure and Expulsion Case from 1789 to 1973, supra; and Maskell, "Discipline of Members," in The Encyclopedia Of The United States Congress, 641-646 (Simon and Schuster 1993).

[59] H. Rept. 96-351, In the Matter Representative Charles C. Diggs, Jr. (1979); 125 CONG. REC. 21584-21592 (July 31, 1979).

[60] H. Rept. 96-930, In the Matter of Representative Charles H. Wilson (1980), H.Res. 660, 96th Cong., 126 CONG. REC. 13801-13820 (June 10, 1980).

[61] H. Rept. 98-295, In the Matter of Representative Gerry E. Studds (1983), 129 Cong. Rec. 20030-20037 (July 20, 1983); and H. Rept. 98- 296, In the Matter of Representative Daniel B. Crane (1983), 129 Cong. Rec. 20021-20030 (JULY 20, 1983).

[62] H.Rept. 111-661, In the Matter of Representative Charles B. Rangel (2010), H.Res. 1737, 111th Cong., 156 CONG. REC. H7891-H7899 (daily ed. December 2, 2010).

[63] See footnote 24 supra. Other Members have also lost their next election before any House action is completed. See footnote 25 supra. As noted, since no recommendation is made by the committees investigating these matters, it cannot be said with certainty what, if any, discipline would have been recommended by the committees, or approved by the House.

[64] Note II Hinds' Precedents, supra at § 1257 (47th Cong., 1st Sess. (1882)); II Hinds' Precedents, supra at § 1666 (39th Cong., 1st Sess. (1866)).

[65] VI Cannon's Precedents, supra at §236 (67th Cong., 1st Sess.).

[66] Deschler's Precedents, supra at Ch. 12, § 16, p. 196 ("a somewhat lesser punitive measure than censure"); see also Cushing, supra at pp. 266-269, for historical context. See now House Committee on Ethics, supra at Rule 24(g).

[67] H.Rept. 94-1364 (1976), In the Matter of Representative Robert L.F. Sikes. No recommendation for punishment was made for an "obvious and significant conflict of interest" – a significant ownership interest in land directly impacted by legislation the Member sponsored, since the "events occurred approximately 15 years ago and ... appear to have been known to [his] constituency.... " Id. at 4-5.

[68] Deschler's Precedents, supra at Ch. 12, § 16, p. 196.

[69] See Appendix.

[70] H.Res. 744, 111th Congress, adopted by the House, September 15, 2009, 155 CONG. REC. H9529-H9534 (daily ed.). The matter was raised by another Member as a privileged resolution.

[71] Deschler's Precedents, supra at Ch. 12, § 17, p. 203. Note, Cushing, supra at § 675.

[72] House Committee on Ethics, Rule 24(e)(4).

[73] 103 U.S. 168 (1880).

[74] 103 U.S. at 189, 190. There is no known case of a congressional imprisonment of a Member in the history of Congress. See discussion in United States v. Traficant, 368 F.3d 646, 651 (6th Cir. 2004): "Congress has not done so, even once, dating back to the year 1787."

[75] In the Senate, in a 1990 disciplinary matter in which a Senator was "denounced" by the full Senate, for example, the Senator was ordered to "reimburse" the Senate a specified amount in connection with questionable expense reimbursements received from the Senate, and "to pay to charities with which he has no affiliation" an amount equal to that which was considered as "excess honoraria" over and above that which the Senator was permitted to accept. S. Rept. 101-382, at 14-15 (1990).

[76] Studies have noted that prior to 1969, no Members of the House had ever been fined for disciplinary reasons. McLaughlin, "Congressional Self-Discipline: The Power to Expel, Exclude and to Punish," 41 Fordham L.R. 43, 61 (Oct. 1972). There had in the 1800's been a few instances noted in precedents where the House authorized fines for absences, or as a condition for discharge. Note, IV Hinds' Precedents, supra at §§ 3011-3014.

[77] H. Res. 2, 91st Cong., 1st Sess., In the Matter of Representative Adam Clayton Powell (1969), note Deschler's Precedents, supra at Ch. 12, §17, pp. 203-204. The Sergeant at Arms was directed to deduct $1,150 a month from the Member's salary.

[78] H.Rept. 96-351, at 20 (1979), In the Matter of Representative Charles Diggs, Jr.

[79] H.Rept. 112-642 (2012), In the Matter of Allegations Relating to Representative Laura Richardson; see adoption of Committee Report and House reprimand, at 158 Cong. Rec. H5635- H3639 (daily ed. August 2, 2012).

[80] H.Rept. 101-610, (1990), In the Matter of Representative Barney Frank.

[81] H.Rept. 105-1, at 3 (1997), In the Matter of Representative Newt Gingrich.

[82] House Committee on Ethics, Rule 24(g).

[83] Id.

[84] Cushing, supra, at section 627, p. 251.

[85] Jefferson's Manual And Rules Of The House Of Representatives, §658. Deschler's Precedents, supra at Ch. 12, § 15, p. 187.

[86] Citations are to volumes of Hinds' And Cannon's Precedents Of The United States House of Representatives, and to the relevant sections.

[87] See now, House Rule XXIII (10); note H.Rept. 93-616, (1973).

[88] 121 CONG. REC. 10341, April 16, 1975, colloquy between Representatives Robert Eckhardt and John J. Flynt of Texas.

[89] House Rule XXIII(2); note comments on passage of abstention rule by Representatives Edwards and Drinan, 121 CONG. REC., supra at 10343-10345, and discussion in Deschler's Precedents, Ch. 12, § 15 (1977).

[90] The committee in 1993 noted in its report that although there is no "specific enforcement capability" expressed in the proposed rule, "any Member subject to its provisions at the time of the resolution's adoption, or thereafter, who violates the clear principles it expresses, will do so at the risk of subjecting himself to the introduction of a privileged

resolution relating to his conduct.... " H.Rept. 93-616, supra at 4. Note, Washington Post, "Under Colleagues' Pressure, Biaggi Refrains from Voting," October 22, 1987. See also House Committee on Standards of Official Conduct, "Dear Colleague" letter from the Chairman and Vice Chairman, April 15, 2002, warning Member convicted of felony violations that "by voting in the House – you risk subjecting yourself to action by this Committee, and by the House, in addition to any other disciplinary action that may be initiated in connection with your criminal conviction."

[91] House Rule XI, para. 3(a)(1).

[92] House Rule XI, para. 3(a)(1) provides that a "letter of reproval or other administrative action of the committee pursuant to an investigation ... shall only be issued ... as part of a report required" under subparagraph (2) of the Rule. Subparagraph (2) states that the Committee on Ethics "shall report to the House its findings of fact and recommendations, if any, upon the final disposition of any such investigation, and such action as the committee may deem appropriate in the circumstances." House Rule XI, para. 3(a)(2).

[93] House Rule XI, para.3(a)(1); House Committee on Ethics, Rule 24(c).

[94] A Letter of Reproval is not one of the "sanctions" recommended to the House, listed in the Committee Rules at Rule 24(e).

[95] House Committee on Ethics, Rule 24(c).

[96] House Committee on Ethics, Rule 24(d).

[97] House Committee on Ethics, Rule 24(b),(c) and (d). See also Committee Rule 26(b), waiver of procedural steps by respondent.

[98] H.Rept. 106-979, at 3J, (2000), In the Matter of Representative E.G. "Bud" Shuster.

[99] H.Rept. 100-382, at 5, 6, (1987), In the Matter of Representative Richard H. Stallings. The committee recommended against sanctions by the full House because of several "mitigating" factors, including "no evidence of improper intent" of the Member either to conceal the activity or to violate the provisions of the Rule as the loans were fully reported on required disclosures, and the voluntary "corrective action" on the Member's own initiative once the Member became aware of the violations.

[100] H.Rept. 100-526, (1988), In the Matter of Representative Charles G. Rose III. The committee cited "mitigating circumstances which prevent these violations from rising to the level of a recommendation of sanction to the full House," and commended the "positive action taken" by the Member. Id. at 26.

[101] H.Rept. 101-293, (1989), In the Matter of Representative Jim Bates. The committee initiated a Preliminary Inquiry and the Member waived his rights to a Statement of Alleged Violations and a disciplinary hearing. The committee noted that since the Member had taken steps to assure no repeat of the offending conduct, was being directed to specifically issue apologies to the affected employees, and that since any inappropriate campaign activities were "sporadic" and not on-going, that "the better course is to formally and publicly reprove" the Member. Id. at 13-14.

[102] H.Rept. 106-979, at 3D-3E (2000), In the Matter of Representative E.G. "Bud" Shuster.

[103] H.Rept. 107-130, (2001), In the Matter of Representative Earl F. Hilliard.

[104] House Committee on Ethics, Rule 24(c).

[105] See H.Rept. 101-995, at 8 (1990), Summary of Activities, One Hundred First Congress; H.Rept. 106-1044, at 11-12 (2001).

[106] H.Rept. 104-401, at 2, 4-5 (1995), Inquiry Into Various Complaints Filed Against Representative Newt Gingrich.

[107] H.Rept. 101-397, at 2, 14 (1990), In the Matter of Representative Gus Savage.

[108] H.Rept. 108-722, at 2 (2004), "Investigation of Allegations Related to Voting on the Medicare Prescription Drug, Improvement, and Modernization Act of 2003," concerning allegations of trading votes on a Medicare measure in return for political support of a Member's relative.

[109] The committee made public the report on December 8, 2006 (109th Cong., 2d Sess.). See H.Rept. 109-744, at 15-16 (2007). The committee also issued a press release concerning a misdemeanor assault charge against a Member towards an airline employee, noting that the investigative subcommittee found that the Member "demonstrated poor judgment," and that such conduct "implicated the reputation of the House of Representatives." H.Rept. 110-938, at 189 (2007).

[110] House Committee on Standards of Official Conduct, Report, "Investigation into Officially Connected Travel of House Members to Attend the Carib News Foundation Multi-National Business Conferences in 2007 and 2008," at p. V (February 25, 2010).

[111] Report Adopted by the Committee on Ethics, December 20, 2012, 112th Cong., 2nd Sess., at 1.

[112] Report, supra at p. 51.

[113] House Ethics Manual, 110th Cong., 2d Sess., at 12 (2008).

[114] Compare committee descriptions at H.Rept. 101-995, supra at 8, and 9; note HOUSE ETHICS MANUAL, supra at 11.

[115] As noted, House Rules provide that a "letter of reproval or other administrative action of the Committee" may be invoked "pursuant to an investigation." House Rule XI, para. 3(a)(1); House Committee on Ethics, Rule 24(c), (d). These other actions, however, do not necessarily require the adoption or proof of a Statement of Alleged Violations. See, for example, Committee Rule 19(g).

[116] See Statement of the Committee on Standards of Official Conduct, October 6, 2004; Memorandum to the Members of the Committee, from the Chairman and Ranking Minority Member, "Recommendations for disposition of the complaint filed against Representative DeLay," and "Dear Colleague" letter to Members, October 6, 2004.

[117] As noted, a "Letter of Reproval" or other committee action would appear to come only after an investigative subcommittee had been convened and had issued a report to the full Committee on Ethics. A Letter of Reproval could follow when a Statement of Alleged Violations is adopted and proved or admitted, and the full committee had then decided by majority vote to "adopt a motion to issue a Letter of Reproval" as sufficient action in lieu of House action (House Committee on Ethics, Rule 24(b),(c)), while other administrative action could apparently be provided by the committee pursuant to an investigation.

[118] House Committee on Ethics, Rule 16(b), (c).

In: U.S. House of Representatives
Editor: Bruno Montagne
ISBN: 978-1-62808-364-4

Chapter 4

ACTIVITIES OF THE COMMITTEE FOR THE 112TH CONGRESS*

U.S. House of Representatives Committee on Ethics

December 31, 2012

HON. KAREN L. HAAS
Clerk, House of Representatives
Washington, DC.

Dear Ms. Haas:

Pursuant to clause 1(d) of Rule XI of the Rules of the House of Representatives, we hereby submit to the House a report on the Activities of the Committee on Ethics for the 112th Congress.

Sincerely,

Jo Bonner
Chairman

Linda T. Sanchez
Ranking Member

---

* This is an edited, reformatted and augmented version of U.S. House of Representatives Committee on Ethics, dated December 31, 2012.

SUMMARY OF ACTIVITIES ONE HUNDRED TWELFTH CONGRESS

December 31, 2012. — Committed to the Committee of the Whole House on the State of the Union and ordered to be printed

Mr. BONNER and Ms. SANCHEZ, from the Committee on Ethics, submitted the following

REPORT

The Committee on Ethics is tasked with interpreting and enforcing the House's ethics rules. The Committee has sole jurisdiction over the interpretation of the Code of Official Conduct, which governs the acts of House Members, officers, and employees. The Committee is the only standing House committee with equal numbers of Democratic and Republican members. The operative staff of the Committee is required by rule to be professional and nonpartisan.

In the 112th Congress the Committee was led by Chairman Jo Bonner and Ranking Member Linda T. Sanchez. The Members appointed at the beginning of the Congress were Michael T. McCaul, John A. Yarmuth, K. Michael Conaway, Donna F. Edwards, Charles W. Dent, Mazie Hirono, Gregg Harper and Pedro R. Pierluisi. In July 2011, Representative Joe Courtney replaced Representative Hirono.

The Committee's core responsibilities include providing training, advice, and education to House Members, officers, and employees; reviewing and approving requests to accept privately-sponsored travel related to official duties; reviewing and certifying all financial disclosure reports Members, candidates and senior staff are required to file; and investigating and adjudicating allegations of misconduct and violations of rules, laws, or other standards of conduct.

The Committee met 51 times in the 112th Congress, including 16 times in 2011, and 35 times in 2012. Every Committee vote in the 112th Congress was unanimous.

Within the scope of its training, advice and education, travel, and financial disclosure responsibilities, the Committee:

- Issued more than 900 formal advisory opinions regarding ethics rules;
- Fielded more than 40,000 informal telephone calls, emails, and in-person requests for guidance on ethics issues;
- Released 23 advisory memoranda on various ethics topics to the House;
- Provided training to approximately 10,000 House Members, officers, and employees each year, and reviewed their certifications for satisfying the House's mandatory training requirements; and
- Received more than 6,000 Financial Disclosure Statements and amendments filed by House Members, officers, senior staff, and House candidates.
- Received approximately 500 Periodic Transaction Reports filed by House Members, officers, and senior staff, containing thousands of transactions.

In addition, the Committee actively investigates allegations against House Members, officers, and employees, using a mix of informal and formal investigative techniques to determine the validity of factual allegations, explore potential rules violations, and recommend appropriate sanctions and corrective actions. The Committee's options for investigating a matter include fact-gathering under Committee Rule 18(a), which may or may not be publicly disclosed, the empanelment of investigative subcommittees, and the review of transmittals from the Office of Congressional Ethics (OCE). The fact that the Committee is investigating a particular matter or that a House Member, officer, or employee is referenced in an investigative matter should not be construed as a finding or suggestion that the Member, officer, or employee has committed any violation of the rules, law, or standards of conduct.

During the 112th Congress, within the scope of its investigative responsibilities, the Committee:

- Commenced or continued investigative fact-gathering regarding 96 separate investigative matters;
- Empanelled 2 new investigative subcommittees, in the matters of Representative Laura Richardson and Representative Shelley Berkley;
- Re-empanelled the investigative subcommittee in matters related to allegations against Former Representative Eric Massa;
- Held 32 investigative subcommittee meetings; Filed 14 reports with the House totaling nearly 1,700 pages regarding various investigative matters;

- Publicly addressed 27 matters, described in Section V of this report;
- Resolved 42 additional matters;
- Conducted 102 voluntary witness interviews;
- Deposed 4 witnesses pursuant to subpoena;
- Authorized the issuance of 9 subpoenas; and
- Reviewed nearly 500,000 pages of documents.

All votes taken in the investigative subcommittees were unanimous. In addition to the publicly-disclosed matters discussed in this report, there were a total of 34 investigative matters pending before the Committee as of December 31, 2012.

I. INTRODUCTION

House Rule XI, clause 1(d), requires each committee to submit to the House, not later than July 1 and December 31 of each year, a report on the activities of that committee under that rule and House Rule X during the Congress ending on January 3 of that year. This report summarizes the activities of the Committee on Ethics for the semiannual period ending December 31, 2012, as well as for the entirety of the 112th Congress.

The jurisdiction of the Committee on Ethics ("Committee") is defined in clauses 1(g) and 11(g)(4) of House Rule X, clause 3 of House Rule XI, and clause 5(h) of House Rule XXV. The text of those provisions is as follows:

Rule X, clause 1(g)

1. There shall be in the House the following standing committees, each of which shall have the jurisdiction and related functions assigned by this clause and clauses 2, 3, and 4.

* * *

(g) Committee on Ethics.
The Code of Official Conduct.

Rule X, clause 11(g)(4)

(4) The Committee on Ethics shall investigate any unauthorized disclosure of intelligence or intelligence-related information by a Member, Delegate, Resident Commissioner, officer, or employee of the House in violation of

subparagraph (3) and report to the House concerning any allegation that it finds to be substantiated.

Rule XI, clause 3

Committee on Ethics

3. (a) The Committee on Ethics has the following functions:

(1) The committee may recommend to the House from time to time such administrative actions as it may consider appropriate to establish or enforce standards of official conduct for Members, Delegates, the Resident Commissioner, officers, and employees of the House. A letter of reproval or other administrative action of the committee pursuant to an investigation under subparagraph (2) shall only be issued or implemented as a part of a report required by such subparagraph.

(2) The committee may investigate, subject to paragraph (b), an alleged violation by a Member, Delegate, Resident Commissioner, officer, or employee of the House of the Code of Official Conduct or of a law, rule, regulation, or other standard of conduct applicable to the conduct of such Member, Delegate, Resident Commissioner, officer, or employee in the performance of the duties or the discharge of the responsibilities of such individual. After notice and hearing (unless the right to a hearing is waived by the Member, Delegate, Resident Commissioner, officer, or employee), the committee shall report to the House its fmdings of fact and recommendations, if any, for the final disposition of any such investigation and such action as the committee may consider appropriate in the circumstances.

(3) The committee may report to the appropriate Federal or State authorities, either with the approval of the House or by an affirmative vote of two-thirds of the members of the committee, any substantial evidence of a violation by a Member, Delegate, Resident Commissioner, officer, or employee of the House, of a law applicable to the performance of his duties or the discharge of the responsibilities of such individual that may have been disclosed in a committee investigation.

(4) The committee may consider the request of a Member, Delegate, Resident Commissioner, officer, or employee of the House for an advisory opinion with respect to the general propriety of any current or proposed conduct of such Member, Delegate, Resident Commissioner, officer, or employee. With appropriate deletions to ensure the privacy of the person concerned, the committee may publish such opinion for the guidance of other Members, Delegates, the Resident Commissioner, officers, and employees of the House.

(5) The committee may consider the request of a Member, Delegate, Resident Commissioner, officer, or employee of the House for a written waiver in exceptional circumstances with respect to clause 4 of rule XXIII.

(6)(A) The committee shall offer annual ethics training to each Member, Delegate, Resident Commissioner, officer, and employee of the House. Such training shall-

(i) involve the classes of employees for whom the committee determines such training to be appropriate; and

(ii) include such knowledge of the Code of Official Conduct and related House rules as may be determined appropriate by the committee.

(B)(i) A new officer or employee of the House shall receive training under this paragraph not later than 60 days after beginning service to the House.

(ii) Not later than January 31 of each year, each officer and employee of the House shall file a certification with the committee that the officer or employee attended ethics training in the last year as established by this subparagraph.

(b)(1)(A) Unless approved by an affirmative vote of a majority of its members, the Committee on Ethics may not report a resolution, report, recommendation, or advisory opinion relating to the official conduct of a Member, Delegate, Resident Commissioner, officer, or employee of the House, or, except as provided in subparagraph (2), undertake an investigation of such conduct.

(B)(i) Upon the receipt of information offered as a complaint that is in compliance with this rule and the rules of the committee, the chair and ranking minority member jointly may appoint members to serve as an investigative subcommittee.

(ii) The chair and ranking minority member of the committee jointly may gather additional information concerning alleged conduct that is the basis of a complaint or of information offered as a complaint until they have established an investigative subcommittee or either of them has placed on the agenda of the committee the issue of whether to establish an investigative subcommittee.

(2) Except in the case of an investigation undertaken by the committee on its own initiative, the committee may undertake an investigation relating to the official conduct of an individual Member, Delegate, Resident Commissioner, officer, or employee of the House only—

(A) upon receipt of information offered as a complaint, in writing and under oath, from a Member, Delegate, or Resident Commissioner and transmitted to the committee by such Member, Delegate, or Resident Commissioner;

(B) upon receipt of information offered as a complaint, in writing and under oath, from a person not a Member, Delegate, or Resident Commissioner provided that a Member, Delegate, or Resident Commissioner certifies in writing to the committee that such Member, Delegate, or Resident Commissioner believes the information is submitted in good faith and warrants the review and consideration of the committee; or

(C) upon receipt of a report regarding a referral from the Office of Congressional Ethics.

If a complaint is not disposed of within the applicable periods set forth in the rules of the Committee on Ethics, the chair and ranking minority member shall establish jointly an investigative subcommittee and forward the complaint, or any portion thereof, to that subcommittee for its consideration. However, if at any time during those periods either the chair or ranking minority member places on the agenda the issue of whether to establish an investigative subcommittee, then an investigative subcommittee may be established only by an affirmative vote of a majority of the members of the committee.

(3) The committee may not undertake an investigation of an alleged violation of a law, rule, regulation, or standard of conduct that was not in effect at the time of the alleged violation. The committee may not undertake an investigation of such an alleged violation that occurred before the third previous Congress unless the committee determines that the alleged violation is directly related to an alleged violation that occurred in a more recent Congress.

(4) A member of the committee shall be ineligible to participate as a member of the committee in a committee proceeding relating to the member's official conduct. Whenever a member of the committee is ineligible to act as a member of the committee under the preceding sentence, the Speaker shall designate a Member, Delegate, or Resident Commissioner from the same political party as the ineligible member to act in any proceeding of the committee relating to that conduct.

(5) A member of the committee may seek disqualification from participating in an investigation of the conduct of a Member, Delegate, Resident Commissioner, officer, or employee of the House upon the submission in writing and under oath of an affidavit of disqualification stating that the member cannot render an impartial and unbiased decision in the case in which the member seeks to be disqualified. If the committee approves and accepts such affidavit of disqualification, the chair shall so notify the Speaker and request the Speaker to designate a Member, Delegate, or Resident

Commissioner from the same political party as the disqualifying member to act in any proceeding of the committee relating to that case.

(6) Information or testimony received, or the contents of a complaint or the fact of its filing, may not be publicly disclosed by any committee or staff member unless specifically authorized in each instance by a vote of the full committee.

(7) The committee shall have the functions designated in titles I and V of the Ethics in Government Act of 1978 [on financial disclosure and the limitations on outside earned income and outside employment], in sections 7342 [the Foreign Gifts and Decorations Act], 7351 [on gifts to superiors], and 7353 [on gifts] of title 5, United States Code, and in clause 11(g)(4) of rule X.

(c)(1) Notwithstanding clause 2(g)(1) of rule XI, each meeting of the Committee on Ethics or a subcommittee thereof shall occur in executive session unless the committee or subcommittee, by an affirmative vote of a majority of its members, opens the meeting to the public.

(2) Notwithstanding clause 2(g)(2) of rule XI, each hearing of an adjudicatory subcommittee or sanction hearing of the Committee on Ethics shall be held in open session unless the committee or subcommittee, in open session by an affirmative vote of a majority of its members, closes all or part of the remainder of the hearing on that day to the public.

(d) Before a member, officer, or employee of the Committee on Ethics, including members of a subcommittee of the committee selected under clause 5(a)(4) of rule X and shared staff, may have access to information that is confidential under the rules of the committee, the following oath (or affirmation) shall be executed:

"I do solemnly swear (or affirm) that I will not disclose, to any person or entity outside the Committee on Ethics, any information received in the course of my service with the committee, except as authorized by the committee or in accordance with its rules."

Copies of the executed oath shall be retained by the Clerk as part of the records of the House. This paragraph establishes a standard of conduct within the meaning of paragraph (a)(2). Breaches of confidentiality shall be investigated by the Committee on Ethics and appropriate action shall be taken.

(e)(1) If a complaint or information offered as a complaint is deemed frivolous by an affirmative vote of a majority of the members of the Committee on Ethics, the committee may take such action as it, by an affirmative vote of a majority of its members, considers appropriate in the circumstances.

(2) Complaints filed before the One Hundred Fifth Congress may not be deemed frivolous by the Committee on Ethics.

Committee agendas

(f) The committee shall adopt rules providing that the chair shall establish the agenda for meetings of the committee, but shall not preclude the ranking minority member from placing any item on the agenda.

Committee staff

(g)(1) The committee shall adopt rules providing that—

(A) the staff be assembled and retained as a professional, nonpartisan staff

(B) each member of the staff shall be professional and demonstrably qualified for the position for which he is hired;

(C) the staff as a whole and each member of the staff shall perform all official duties in a nonpartisan manner;

(D) no member of the staff shall engage in any partisan political activity directly affecting any congressional or presidential election;

(E) no member of the staff or outside counsel may accept public speaking engagements or write for publication on any subject that is in any way related to the employment or duties with the committee of such individual without specific prior approval from the chair and ranking minority member; and

(F) no member of the staff or outside counsel may make public, unless approved by an affirmative vote of a majority of the members of the committee, any information, document, or other material that is confidential, derived from executive session, or classified and that is obtained during the course of employment with the committee.

(2) Only subdivisions (C), (E), and (F) of subparagraph (1) shall apply to shared staff.

(3)(A) All staff members shall be appointed by an affirmative vote of a majority of the members of the committee. Such vote shall occur at the first meeting of the membership of the committee during each Congress and as necessary during the Congress.

(B) Subject to the approval of the Committee on House Administration, the committee may retain counsel not employed by the House of Representatives whenever the committee determines, by an affirmative vote of a majority of the members of the committee, that the retention of outside counsel is necessary and appropriate.

(C) If the committee determines that it is necessary to retain staff members for the purpose of a particular investigation or other proceeding, then such staff shall be retained only for the duration of that particular investigation or proceeding.

(D) Outside counsel may be dismissed before the end of a contract between the committee and such counsel only by an affirmative vote of a majority of the members of the committee.

(4) In addition to any other staff provided for by law, rule, or other authority, with respect to the committee, the chair and ranking minority member each may appoint one individual as a shared staff member from the respective personal staff of the chair or ranking minority member to perform service for the committee. Such shared staff may assist the chair or ranking minority member on any subcommittee on which the chair or ranking minority member serves.

Meetings and hearings

(h)(1) The committee shall adopt rules providing that—

(A) all meetings or hearings of the committee or any subcommittee thereof, other than any hearing held by an adjudicatory subcommittee or any sanction hearing held by the committee, shall occur in executive session unless the committee or subcommittee by an affirmative vote of a majority of its members opens the meeting or hearing to the public; and

(B) any hearing held by an adjudicatory subcommittee or any sanction hearing held by the committee shall be open to the public unless the committee or subcommittee by an affirmative vote of a majority of its members closes the hearing to the public.

Public disclosure

(i) The committee shall adopt rules providing that, unless otherwise determined by a vote of the committee, only the chair or ranking minority member, after consultation with each other, may make public statements regarding matters before the committee or any subcommittee thereof.

Requirements to constitute a complaint

(j) The committee shall adopt rules regarding complaints to provide that whenever information offered as a complaint is submitted to the committee, the chair and ranking minority member shall have 14 calendar days or five legislative days, whichever is sooner, to determine whether the information meets the requirements of the rules of the committee for what constitutes a complaint.

Duties of chair and ranking minority member regarding properly filed complaints

(k)(1) The committee shall adopt rules providing that whenever the chair and ranking minority member jointly determine that information submitted to the committee meets the requirements of the rules of the committee for what constitutes a complaint, they shall have 45 calendar days or five legislative days, whichever is later, after that determination (unless the committee by an affirmative vote of a majority of its members votes otherwise) to—

(A) recommend to the committee that it dispose of the complaint, or any portion thereof, in any manner that does not require action by the House, which may include dismissal of the complaint or resolution of the complaint by a letter to the Member, officer, or employee of the House against whom the complaint is made;

(B) establish an investigative subcommittee; or

(C) request that the committee extend the applicable 45-calendar day or five-legislative day period by one additional 45-calendar day period when they determine more time is necessary in order to make a recommendation under subdivision (A).

(2) The committee shall adopt rules providing that if the chair and ranking minority member jointly determine that information submitted to the committee meets the requirements of the rules of the committee for what constitutes a complaint, and the complaint is not disposed of within the applicable time periods under subparagraph (1), then they shall establish an investigative subcommittee and forward the complaint, or any portion thereof, to that subcommittee for its consideration. However, if, at any time during those periods, either the chair or ranking minority member places on the agenda the issue of whether to establish an investigative subcommittee, then an investigative subcommittee may be established only by an affirmative vote of a majority of the members of the committee.

Duties of chair and ranking minority member regarding information not constituting a complaint

(l) The committee shall adopt rules providing that whenever the chair and ranking minority member jointly determine that information submitted to the committee does not meet the requirements of the rules of the committee for what constitutes a complaint, they may—

(1) return the information to the complainant with a statement that it fails to meet the requirements of the rules of the committee for what constitutes a complaint; or

(2) recommend to the committee that it authorize the establishment of an investigative subcommittee.

Investigative and adjudicatory subcommittees

(m) The committee shall adopt rules providing that—

(1)(A) an investigative subcommittee shall be composed of four Members (with equal representation from the majority and minority parties) whenever such a subcommittee is established pursuant to the rules of the committee;

(B) an adjudicatory subcommittee shall be composed of the members of the committee who did not serve on the pertinent investigative subcommittee (with equal representation from the majority and minority parties) whenever such a subcommittee is established pursuant to the rules of the committee; and

(C) notwithstanding any other provision of this clause, the chair and ranking minority member of the committee may consult with an investigative subcommittee either on their own initiative or on the initiative of the subcommittee, shall have access to information before a subcommittee with which they so consult, and shall not thereby be precluded from serving as full, voting members of any adjudicatory subcommittee;

(2) at the time of appointment, the chair shall designate one member of a subcommittee to serve as chair and the ranking minority member shall designate one member of the subcommittee to serve as the ranking minority member; and

(3) the chair and ranking minority member of the committee may serve as members of an investigative subcommittee, but may not serve as non-voting, ex officio members.

Standard of proof for adoption of statement of alleged violation

(n) The committee shall adopt rules to provide that an investigative subcommittee may adopt a statement of alleged violation only if it determines by an affirmative vote of a majority of the members of the subcommittee that there is substantial reason to believe that a violation of the Code of Official Conduct, or of a law, rule, regulation, or other standard of conduct applicable to the performance of official duties or the discharge of official responsibilities by a Member, officer, or employee of the House of Representatives, has occurred.

Subcommittee powers

(o)(1) The committee shall adopt rules providing that an investigative subcommittee or an adjudicatory subcommittee may authorize and issue subpoenas only when authorized by an affirmative vote of a majority of the members of the subcommittee.

(2) The committee shall adopt rules providing that an investigative subcommittee may, upon an affirmative vote of a majority of its members, expand the scope of its investigation approved by an affninative vote of a majority of the members of the committee.

(3) The committee shall adopt rules to provide that—

an investigative subcommittee may, upon an affirmative vote of a majority of its members, amend its statement of alleged violation anytime before the statement of alleged violation is transmitted to the committee; and

(B) if an investigative subcommittee amends its statement of alleged violation, the respondent shall be notified in writing and shall have 30 calendar days from the date of that notification to file an answer to the amended statement of alleged violation.

Due process rights of respondents

(p) The committee shall adopt rules to provide that—

(1) not less than 10 calendar days before a scheduled vote by an investigative subcommittee on a statement of alleged violation, the subcommittee shall provide the respondent with a copy of the statement of alleged violation it intends to adopt together with all evidence it intends to use to prove those charges which it intends to adopt, including documentary evidence, witness testimony, memoranda of witness interviews, and physical evidence, unless the subcommittee by an affirmative vote of a majority of its members decides to withhold certain evidence in order to protect a witness; but if such evidence is withheld, the subcommittee shall inform the respondent that evidence is being withheld and of the count to which such evidence relates;

(2) neither the respondent nor the counsel of the respondent shall, directly or indirectly, contact the subcommittee or any member thereof during the period of time set forth in paragraph (1) except for the sole purpose of settlement discussions where counsel for the respondent and the subcommittee are present;

(3) if, at any time after the issuance of a statement of alleged violation, the committee or any subcommittee thereof determines that it intends to use evidence not provided to a respondent under paragraph (1) to prove the charges contained in the statement of alleged violation (or any amendment thereof), such evidence shall be made immediately available to the respondent, and it may be used in any further proceeding under the rules of the committee;

(4) evidence provided pursuant to paragraph (1) or (3) shall be made available to the respondent and the counsel of the respondent only after each agrees, in writing, that no document, information, or other materials obtained pursuant to that paragraph shall be made public until—

(A) such time as a statement of alleged violation is made public by the committee if the respondent has waived the adjudicatory hearing; or

(B) the commencement of an adjudicatory hearing if the respondent has not waived an adjudicatory hearing; but the failure of respondent and the counsel of the respondent to so agree in writing, and their consequent failure to receive the evidence, shall not preclude the issuance of a statement of alleged violation at the end of the period referred to in paragraph (1);

(5) a respondent shall receive written notice whenever—

(A) the chair and ranking minority member determine that information the committee has received constitutes a complaint;

(B) a complaint or allegation is transmitted to an investigative subcommittee;

(C) an investigative subcommittee votes to authorize its first subpoena or to take testimony under oath, whichever occurs first; or

(D) an investigative subcommittee votes to expand the scope of its investigation;

(6) whenever an investigative subcommittee adopts a statement of alleged violation and a respondent enters into an agreement with that subcommittee to settle a complaint on which that statement is based, that agreement, unless the respondent requests otherwise, shall be in writing and signed by the respondent and respondent's counsel, the chair and ranking minority member of the subcommittee, and the outside counsel, if any;

(7) statements or information derived solely from a respondent or the counsel of a respondent during any settlement discussions between the committee or a subcommittee thereof and the respondent shall not be included in any report of the subcommittee or the committee or otherwise publicly disclosed without the consent of the respondent; and

(8) whenever a motion to establish an investigative subcommittee does not prevail, the committee shall promptly send a letter to the respondent informing the respondent of such vote.

Committee reporting requirements

(q) The committee shall adopt rules to provide that—

(1) whenever an investigative subcommittee does not adopt a statement of alleged violation and transmits a report to that effect to the committee, the

committee may by an affirmative vote of a majority of its members transmit such report to the House of Representatives;

(2) whenever an investigative subcommittee adopts a statement of alleged violation, the respondent admits to the violations set forth in such statement, the respondent waives the right to an adjudicatory hearing, and the respondent's waiver is approved by the committee—

(A) the subcommittee shall prepare a report for transmittal to the committee, a final draft of which shall be provided to the respondent not less than 15 calendar days before the subcommittee votes on whether to adopt the report;

(B) the respondent may submit views in writing regarding the fmal draft to the subcommittee within seven calendar days of receipt of that draft;

(C) the subcommittee shall transmit a report to the committee regarding the statement of alleged violation together with any views submitted by the respondent pursuant to subdivision (B), and the committee shall make the report together with the respondent's views available to the public before the commencement of any sanction hearing; and

(D) the committee shall by an affirmative vote of a majority of its members issue a report and transmit such report to the House of Representatives, together with the respondent's views previously submitted pursuant to subdivision (B) and any additional views respondent may submit for attachment to the final report; and

(3) members of the committee shall have not less than 72 hours to review any report transmitted to the committee by an investigative subcommittee before both the commencement of a sanction hearing and the committee vote on whether to adopt the report.

House Rule XXV, clause 5(h)

(h) All the provisions of this clause [the gift rule] shall be interpreted and enforced solely by the Committee on Ethics. The Committee on Ethics is authorized to issue guidance on any matter contained in this clause.

In addition, a number of provisions of statutory law confer authority on the Committee. Specifically, for purposes of the statutes on gifts to federal employees (5 U.S.C. § 7353) and gifts to superiors (5 U.S.C. § 7351), both the Committee and the House of Representatives are the "supervising ethics office" of House Members, officers, and employees. In addition, as discussed further in Part III below, for House Members, officers, and employees, the Committee is both the "supervising ethics office" with regard to financial disclosure under the Ethics in Government Act (5 U.S.C. app. 4 § 101 *et seq.)* and the "employing agency" for certain purposes under the Foreign Gifts and Decorations Act (5 U.S.C. § 7342). Finally, the outside employment and earned income limitations are administered by the Committee with respect to House Members, officers, and employees (5 U.S.C. app. 4 § 503(1)(A)).

II. ADVICE AND EDUCATION

Pursuant to a provision of the Ethics Reform Act of 1989 (2 U.S.C. § 29d(i)), the Committee maintains an Office of Advice and Education, which is staffed as directed by the Committee's Chairman and Ranking Member. Under the statute, the primary responsibilities of the Office include the following:

- Providing information and guidance to House Members, officers, and employees on the laws, rules, and other standards of conduct applicable to them in their official capacities;
- Drafting responses to specific advisory opinion requests received from House Members, officers, and employees, and submitting them to the Chairman and Ranking Member for review and approval;
- Drafting advisory memoranda on the ethics rules for general distribution to House Members, officers, and employees, and submitting them to the Chairman and Ranking Member, or the full Committee, for review and approval; and
- Developing and conducting educational briefings for House Members, officers, and employees.

The duties of the Office of Advice and Education are also addressed in Committee Rule 3, which sets out additional requirements and procedures for the issuance of Committee advisory opinions.

Under Committee Rule 3(j), the Committee will keep confidential any request for advice from a Member, officer, or employee, as well as any response to such a request. As a further inducement to House Members, officers, and employees to seek Committee advice whenever they have any uncertainty on the applicable laws, rules, or standards, statutory law (2 U.S.C. § 29d(i)(4)) provides that no information provided to the Committee by a Member or staff person when seeking advice on prospective conduct may be used as a basis for initiating a Committee investigation if the individual acts in accordance with the Committee's written advice. In the same vein, Committee

Rule 3(k) provides that the Committee may take no adverse action in regard to any conduct that has been undertaken in reliance on a written opinion of the Committee if the conduct conforms to the specific facts addressed in the opinion. In addition, the Committee understands that federal courts may consider the good faith reliance of a House Member, officer, or employee on written Committee advice as a defense to Justice Department prosecution regarding certain statutory violations.

The Committee believes that a broad, active program for advice and education is an extremely important means for attaining understanding of and compliance with, the ethics rules. The specifics of the Committee's efforts in the areas of publications, briefings, and advisory opinion letters during the 112th Congress are set forth below. In addition, on a daily basis Committee staff attorneys provided informal advice in response to inquiries received from Members, staff persons, and third parties in telephone calls and e-mails directed to the Committee office, as well as in person. During the 112th Congress, Committee attorneys responded to more than 40,000 phone calls and e-mail messages seeking advice, and participated in many informal meetings with Members, House staff, or outside individuals or groups regarding specific ethics matters.

PUBLICATIONS

The Committee's major publication is the *House Ethics Manual,* an updated version of which was issued in March 2008. The Manual provides detailed explanations of all aspects of the ethics rules and statutes applicable to House Members, officers, and employees. Topics covered by the Manual include the acceptance of gifts or travel, campaign activity, casework, outside employment, and involvement with official and outside organizations. The *House Ethics Manual* is posted in a searchable format on the Committee's Web site, http://ethics.house.gov.

The Committee updates and expands upon the materials in the Manual, as well as highlights matters of particular concern, through the issuance of general advisory memoranda to all House Members, officers, and employees. The memoranda issued during the 112th Congress (other than ones announcing training dates) were as follows:

- New Employee Mandatory Ethics Training within 60 days (January 25, 2011);
- The 2011 Outside Earned Income Limit and Salaries Triggering the Financial Disclosure Requirement and Post-Employment Restrictions Applicable to House Officers and Employees (February 5, 2011);
- Calendar Year 2010 Financial Disclosure Statements (April 6, 2011);
- Committee on Ethics and Committee on House Administration Joint Guidance Regarding Redistricting (September 16, 2011);
- Rules Regarding Personal Financial Transactions (November 29, 2011);
- Holiday Guidance on the Gift Rule (December 9, 2011);
- Revised Legal Expense Fund Regulations (December 20, 2011);
- Member Participation in Certain Events Taking Place During a National Political Convention (January 24, 2012);
- The 2012 Outside Earned Income Limit and Salaries Triggering the Financial Disclosure Requirement and Post-Employment Restrictions Applicable to House Officers and Employees (January 30, 2012);
- Change in Rules Regarding Providing a Hyperlink from Campaign Internet Sites to Official Internet Sites (March 9, 2012);
- New Ethics Requirements Resulting from the STOCK Act (April 4, 2012);
- Gift Rules Applicable to National Political Conventions (June 1, 2012);
- Periodic Reporting of Personal Financial Transactions Pursuant to the STOCK Act (June 7, 2012) superseded by revised memorandum following amendment of the STOCK Act (August 17, 2012);
- Purchase of Tablet Computers with Principal Campaign Committee Funds (September 18, 2012);
- REMINDER: Spouse PTR Transaction Reporting Begins September 30, 2012 (September 28, 2012);
- Reminder About the 2012 Annual Ethics Training Requirement (November 21, 2012);
- Negotiations for Future Employment and Restrictions on Post-Employment for House Members and Officers (November 26, 2012);
- Negotiations for Future Employment and Restrictions on Post-Employment for House Staff (November 26, 2012);
- Holiday Guidance on the Gift Rule (November 27, 2012);
- Member Swearing-in and Inauguration Day Receptions, and Attendance at Inaugural-Related Events (December 4, 2012);

- Rules Prohibiting Use of One's Official Position for Personal Gain (December 27, 2012); and
- Revised Travel Regulations (December 27, 2012)

Committee Report (numbers are approximate)	2011	2012	TOTAL
Formal Advice and Approval			
Advisory Opinion Requests Received	597	409	1,006
Advisory Opinions Mailed	535	379	914
Percentage of Opinions Mailed within 2 weeks	64.11%	60.15%	62.13%
Percentage of Opinions Mailed within 4 weeks	80.93%	78.10%	79.52%
Travel Requests Received	2,001	1,563	3,564
Travel Opinions Mailed	1,768	1,379	3,147
Percentage of Travel Opinions Mailed within 2 weeks	63.52%	49.53%	56.53%
Percentage of Travel Opinions Mailed within 4 weeks	91.91%	86.36%	89.14%
Informal Advice (including Financial Disclosure)			
Phone Calls	18,054	18,000	36,054
Emails	3,574	3,000	6,574
Training			
Total # of House Employees	10,000	10,000	10,000
Employees having completed training	9,610	8,500	18,110
Training briefings (scheduled training sessions)	51	42	93
Personal Advisory Meetings with Members, officers, and employees	386	400	786
Investigations			
Investigative Matters carried over from the 111th Congress	23	----	23
Investigative Matters commenced	29	44	73
Investigative Subcommittees carried over from the 111th Congress	1	----	1
Investigative Subcommittees commenced	1	1	2
Publicly Disclosed Resolutions	8	12	20
Confidential Resolutions	4	38	42
Referrals received from the Office of Congressional Ethics	9	13	22
Financial Disclosures			
FD Reports filed by Members, officers, and employees	2,701	2,194	4,895
FD Reports filed by Candidates	434	841	1,275
PTRs filed by Members, officers, and employees	----	500	500
FD Reports and amendments reviewed by Committee staff	3,110	3,635	6,745
Committee Publications			
Pink Sheets/General Advisories	11	17	28
Public Statements	18	28	46
Investigative Reports	7	7	14
Miscellaneous Oversight			
Recusals (Members, officers, and employees)	62	51	113
Negotiations (Only MEMBERS had to disclose publicly, and only if a recusal was necessary)	83	135	218
Qualified Blind Trusts	3	3	3
Legal Expense Funds	7	7	8
Foreign Gifts and Travel Reports	6	0	6
Meetings			
Full Committee Meetings	16	35	51
Subcommittee Meetings	5	27	32
Working Group Meetings	8	9	17
Personnel			
Lowest Total Staff Level	17	23	17
Highest Total Staff Level	24	24	24

In addition to the advisory memoranda listed above, the Committee issued an updated version of its summary memorandum, Highlights of the House

Ethics Rules, in March 2011 and January 2012. The Committee released 46 public statements regarding various matters.

In order to make access to all Committee materials easier and more transparent, the Committee launched a new Web site in the fall of 2011, featuring easily accessible guidance, forms, and historical documents. Significantly, the Committee has now, for the first time, made all conduct reports dating back to the Committee's founding in 1967 available to the public in electronic fon˜n. All of these reports are now available in searchable format on the Committee's Web site. In addition, the Committee is currently working to update the summary of all reported matters of conduct in the entire history of the House of Representatives. Currently that chart ends with 2004. With the launch of the new Web site, the Committee has listened to transparency suggestions and concerns from numerous House and outside sources and continues to make improvements to the usefulness of its Web site.

Copies of all current Committee publications are available from the Committee's office, and their text is posted on the Committee's Web site. Finally, with this report and the annual report published by the Committee in early 2012, the Committee has sought to provide as much transparency as is appropriate. In addition to the many numbers referred to throughout this report, the Committee annually publishes the following summary chart in the interest of transparency.

ETHICS TRAINING

Clause 3(a)(6) of House Rule XI, which originated in the 110th Congress, requires each House employee to complete ethics training each calendar year, pursuant to guidelines to be issued by the Committee. The House rules and Committee's guidelines require each House employee to complete one hour of ethics training each calendar year. The guidelines also require all House employees who file an annual Financial Disclosure Statement to complete an additional hour of training once each Congress on issues primarily of interest to senior staff Rule XI requires staff newly hired by the House to complete their training within 60 days of the commencement of their employment with the House.

Pursuant to its obligations under Rule XI, the Committee held 51 ethics training sessions during 2011 and 42 during 2012. During the 112th Congress, all employees other than new employees were permitted to fulfill their training requirement either through attending a training session in person or by viewing an on-line presentation. The training sessions for new employees provided a general summary of the House ethics rules in all areas, such as gifts, travel, campaign activity, casework, involvement with outside entities, and outside employment. The live and on-line sessions for existing House employees covered specific topics, such as gifts and travel or campaign work, on a more in-depth basis. The Committee also had several different options that staff could use to fulfill their requirement of one additional hour of training. The on-line training provided a general overview of ethics rules of particular interest to senior staff The live training sessions focused in depth on a single topic, of import for senior staff, such as the rules on completing a Financial Disclosure Statement, the post-employment restrictions, or STOCK Act filings.

In 2011, the Committee trained more than 2,400 employees in person at live ethics briefings, and more than 7,500 used one of the on-line training options. During 2012, the Committee trained more than 1,600 employees in person at live ethics briefings, and more than 6,500 through one of the on-line training options. The total number of employees who completed ethics training for 2012 will be determined after January 31, 2013, the date that House Rule XI established as the deadline for employees to certify completion of the ethics training requirement for 2012.

In addition to the training required under House Rule XI, the Committee also provided training in several other contexts. The Committee made three presentations to the Members-elect of the 113th Congress during New Member Orientation for the members-elect of the 113th Congress. The Committee also led a briefing for the spouses of the Members-elect of the 113th Congress on the ethics rules applicable to them as congressional spouses. In addition, the Committee met with numerous departing Members and staff to counsel them on the ethics rules related to their transition to private life and the post-employment restrictions. The Committee also provided training open to all House Members, officers, and employees on the financial disclosure rules, which is discussed further in Section III. Finally, together with the Committee on House Administration, the Committee participated in two general briefings, one in 2011 and one in 2012, on the rules related to Member participation in the Congressional Art Competition.

Committee staff also participated in approximately 10 briefings sponsored by or held for the members of outside organizations. The Committee also had an information booth at the 2011 House Services Fair held by the Chief Administrative Officer. In addition, Committee staff led approximately twelve briefings for visiting international dignitaries from a variety of countries, including Indonesia, China, Moldova, and Romania.

The Committee will continue this outreach activity in the 113th Congress.

ADVISORY OPINION LETTERS

The Committee's Office of Advice and Education, under the direction and supervision of the Committee's Chairman and Ranking Member, prepared and issued more than 900 private advisory opinions during the 112th Congress, 535 in 2011 and more than 375 in 2012. Opinions issued by the Committee in the 112th Congress addressed a wide range of subjects, including various provisions of the gift rule, Member or staff participation in fund-raising activities of charities and for other purposes, the outside earned income and employment limitations, campaign activity by staff, and the post-employment restrictions.

TRAVEL APPROVAL LETTERS

As discussed above, House Rule XXV, clause 5(d)(2), which was enacted at the start of the 110th Congress, charged each House Member or employee with obtaining approval of the Committee prior to undertaking any travel paid for by a private source on matters connected to the individual's House duties. Under the travel approval process established by the Committee to implement this rule, the Committee reviewed more than 2,000 requests, and issued letters approving more than 1,760 requests for travel in 2011. In 2012, the Committee reviewed more than 1,500 requests and issued letters approving more than 1,300 requests for travel. The Committee also reviewed the post-travel disclosure forms filed by the traveler on each approved trip pursuant to House Rule XXV, clause 5(b)(1)(A)(ii), requesting amendments or other remedial action by the traveler when deemed necessary.

House Rule XXV, clause 5(i), charges the Committee with undertaking an annual review of its guidelines and regulations regarding privately-funded, officially-connected travel by House Members, officers, and employees. In 2011, the Committee carried over a bipartisan travel working group to assess and make recommendations regarding its process for the review and approval of such travel. Committee members Representatives Charles Dent and Donna

F. Edwards comprised the working group. As a result of the efforts of the working group, the Committee adopted comprehensive revised travel regulations for privately-sponsored, officially-connected travel which were released as a general advisory on December 27, 2012.

III. FINANCIAL DISCLOSURE, FOREIGN GIFTS & DECORATIONS, AND TRAVEL DISCLOSURE

Title I of the Ethics in Government Act of 1978 (EIGA), as amended (5 U.S.C. app. 4 §§ 101-111), requires certain officials in all branches of the federal government, as well as candidates for federal office, to file publicly-available statements that set out financial information regarding themselves and their families. By May 15 of each year, these "covered individuals" are required to file a statement that provides information for the preceding calendar year. On April 4, 2012, the Stop Trading on Congressional Knowledge Act (STOCK Act) was enacted. Among other provisions, the STOCK Act amended the EIGA to add a requirement that financial disclosure filers must report certain securities transactions over $1,000 within 45 days of the transaction. The Committee has termed these interim reports "Periodic Transaction Reports" or "PTRs."

The EIGA designates the Committee as the "supervising ethics office" of House Members, officers, and employees for purposes of financial disclosure and provides that the Committee is to administer the Act with regard to those individuals. In this role, the Committee interprets the EIGA, establishes policy, issues instructions, and designs the Financial Disclosure Statements (FD Statements or Statements) and PTRs to be filed by Members, officers, legislative branch employees, and candidates for the House. After Statements and PTRs are filed with the Clerk of the House, they are forwarded to the Committee to be reviewed for compliance with the law. For several months each year, accountants from the General Accounting Office assist the Committee in its review efforts. As noted above, in the 112th Congress the Committee received nearly 500 PTRs filed by House Members, officers, and senior staff containing thousands of transactions. The Committee anticipates this figure will increase substantially in the future because the requirement for filing PTRs was only in effect for the second half of 2012, and the inclusion of spouses' and independent children's transactions was only required for approximately the last quarter of 2012.

Each year the Committee publishes two detailed financial disclosure instruction booklets, one for current Members and employees, and one for candidates and new employees. The Committee also published a detailed advisory memorandum providing instructions for completion of a PTR, which was updated following amendment of the Act in August 2012. The appropriate FD instruction booklet and the PTR advisory memorandum are sent to each person who is required to file an FD Statement and PTRs with the Clerk of the House pursuant to House payroll data. Candidates who are required to file FD statements, as determined by records from the Federal Election Commission, are also sent the appropriate FD instructions and forms.

The Committee also engaged in substantial training efforts regarding completing FD Statements and PTRs. Prior to the May 15 filing date, the Committee held six briefings in 2011, three for Members and three for officers and employees, and five briefings in 2012, one for Members, one for Members' spouses, and three for officers and employees, on the financial disclosure requirements. In 2012, the Committee held six briefings on the new PTR requirement, two for Members and four for officers and employees. The Committee issued three advisory memoranda providing guidance to the House community on these new requirements. The Committee staff also met on an individual basis with any Member who had questions regarding the preparation of the Member's Statement or PTR and who requested additional guidance. In addition, Committee staff responded, by telephone, e-mail, or in person, to numerous questions from filers on the financial disclosure filing requirements. Upon request, Committee staff reviewed Statements and PTRs in draft form, prior to being formally filed with the Clerk, for compliance with the disclosure requirements in order to reduce errors and the need for amendments. The Committee encourages all financial disclosure filers to avail themselves of this service for their future filings.

For calendar years 2011 and 2012 (as of December 20, 2012), the Legislative Resource Center of the Clerk's office referred a total of 6,170 Financial Disclosure Statements to the Committee for review under the statute. Of those, 4,183 were Statements filed by current or new House Members or employees, 712 were filed by departing House Members or employees, and 1,275 were Statements filed by candidates for the House. Where the Committee's review indicated that a filed Statement had a deficiency, such as a failure to include required information, the Committee requested an amendment from the filer. Such amendments are routine and, without evidence of a knowing or willful violation, the Committee will usually take no further action.

The Committee also followed up with filers whose Statements indicated non-compliance with applicable law, such as the outside employment and outside earned income limitations. Where the Committee found that a Member or staff person had received income in violation of any of these limitations, the Committee determined the appropriate remedy for the violation, which in some circumstances was a requirement that the individual repay the amount that was improperly received.

For calendar year 2012 (as of December 20, 2012), the Legislative Resource Center of the Clerk's office referred a total of 477 PTRs to the Committee for review under the statute beginning on the effective date of the PTR requirement, July 3, 2012. Of those, 141 were PTRs filed by Members and 336 were PTRs filed by House employees. The Committee has continued to receive a large number of year-end PTRs since the numbers above were compiled.

Like FD Statements, where the Committee's review indicated that a filed PTR had a deficiency, such as a failure to include required information, the Committee requested an amendment from the filer. The Committee also followed up with filers whose PTRs indicated noncompliance with applicable law, such as impermissible participation in an Initial Public Offering or late filing of the PTR. Where the Committee found that a Member or staff person had violated a provision of the STOCK Act, the Committee determined the appropriate remedy for the violation.

IV. COMMITTEE RULES

On February 15, 2011, the Committee met and adopted the initial set of Committee rules for the 112th Congress. The substance of the initial set of Committee rules was largely identical to those adopted for the 111th Congress, except they were changed to reflect the Committee's new name, in conformance with changes that had been made to the House rules for the 112th Congress. Subsequently, on May 18, 2012, the Committee met and adopted a revised set of Committee rules. The May 2012 revisions amended Committee Rule 4 to authorize the Committee to review periodic transaction reports as required by the Stop Trading On Congressional Knowledge (STOCK) Act, and amended Committee Rule 9 to change the quorum requirements of the Committee for the purpose of taking testimony or receiving evidence, from six to two Members. Copies of the February 2011 and amended May 2012

Committee rules are included as Appendices II and III, respectively, to this Report.

On July 7, 2011, the Committee formed a working group to assess the Committee's rules and procedures. The rules working group issued a report to the Committee on November 15, 2012. The rules working group's report suggested various changes to the Committee rules, primarily focused on the Committee's investigative and adjudicative procedures. As a result of the efforts of the working group, the Committee met and adopted new Committee rules on December 19, 2012. Numerous changes were made to the Committee's investigative rules at that time, including changes to Committee rules 17A, 18, 19 and 23. These changes were made either to bring the Committee rules in greater conformity with the House Rules, or to make the Committee's adjudicatory process more fair and efficient.

V. INVESTIGATIONS

Article 1, Section 5 of the Constitution grants each chamber of Congress the power to "punish its Members for disorderly Behaviour, and, with the Concurrence of two thirds, expel a Member." The Committee is designated by House Rule as the body which conducts the investigative and adjudicatory functions which usually precede a vote by the full House regarding such punishment or expulsion. House Rule XI, Clause 3, as well as Committee Rules 13 through 28, describe specific guidelines and procedures for the exercise of that authority.

Beginning prior to the current Congress, allegations had been raised that the public caseload of the Committee represented a racial disparity that was not in line with the general population of the House of Representatives. In the 112th Congress, under the leadership of the Chairman and Ranking Member, the Committee sought to take those allegations seriously, through study and discussion. The Committee began with the understanding that the public caseload, most of which had begun in prior congresses, consisted almost entirely of matters required to be made public as they were referred by the Office of Congressional Ethics. However, the Committee did not rest on that fact alone. In fact, many investigative matters pending before the Committee may not be publicly disclosed. The Committee, therefore, considered the broader but necessarily confidential caseload, which did not reflect the same alleged disparity. The Committee as a whole had several collegial discussions and the staff took steps to ensure they are aware of the potential for bias, and that they remain vigilant to ensure that every case is handled only on the merits and is consistent, in relevant ways, with House and Committee precedent. No matter these numbers, however, the Chairman, Ranking Member, and the entire Committee remained absolutely committed to insuring integrity in the Committee's operations and fairness to the entire House community.

The Committee publicly addressed 27 investigative matters during the 112th Congress.

On September 1, 2010, and November 3, 2010, the Committee received referrals in three matters from the Office of Congressional Ethics (OCE) related to alleged improper fundraising activities and the House vote on H.R. 4173, by Representatives John Campbell, Tom Price, and Joseph Crowley, which was resolved by the Chairman and Ranking Member in the 112th Congress by releasing a staff report on January 26, 2011.

On May 18, 2011, the Committee received a referral from the OCE related to the alleged receipt of an impermissible gift by Representative Jean Schmidt.

On May 18, 2011, the Committee received a referral from the OCE related to the alleged receipt of an improper loan by Representative Gregory Meeks.

On May 18, 2011, the Committee received a referral from the OCE related to the alleged receipt of excess outside earned income by Michael Collins

On May 18, 2011, the Committee received a referral from the OCE related to the alleged receipt of excess outside earned income by Gregory Hill.

On July 14, 2011, the Committee voted to reauthorize the Investigative Subcommittee for the 112th Congress that had been authorized during the 111th Congress in matters related to allegations against former Representative Eric Massa.

On July 20, 2011, the Committee voted to hire outside counsel to review, advise, and assist the Committee in the matter of Representative Maxine Waters.

On August 1, 2011, the Committee voted not to establish an Investigative Subcommittee with regard to the arrest of Representative Luis V. Gutierrez for failing to obey a lawful order of a police officer during a protest outside the White House.

On September 8, 2011, the Committee voted not to establish an Investigative Subcommittee with regard to the arrest of Todd Poole, an employee of the House, for driving while impaired and resisting an officer.

On October 13, 2011, after the withdrawal of a request for deferral from the Department of Justice, the Committee voted to end the deferral period in the matter of Representative Jesse Jackson, Jr., related to allegations that

Representative Jackson, or an agent of Representative Jackson, may have offered to raise funds for then-Illinois Governor Rod Blagojevich in return for the appointment of Representative Jackson to the Illinois Senate seat vacated by President Barack Ob ama.

On October 13, 2011, the Committee received a referral from the OCE related to allegations of improper contributions to Representative Don Young's Legal Expense Fund.

On October 13, 2011, the Committee received a referral from the OCE related to alleged employment discrimination, unwelcome sexual advances, and unwelcome sexual conduct by Representative Alcee L. Hastings.

On November 3, 2011, the Committee voted to establish an Investigative Subcomi¯nittee to investigate the alleged improper use of official House resources and personnel for work related to campaign activities and other non-official purposes by Representative Laura Richardson and two members of her staff.

On November 8, 2011, the Committee received a referral from the OCE related to the alleged failure to report certain positions and unearned income on Financial Disclosure Statements by Representative Vern Buchanan.

On February 9, 2012, the Committee received a referral from the OCE related to allegations that Representative Vern Buchanan attempted to influence the testimony of a witness in a proceeding before the Federal Election Commission.

On February 9, 2012, the Committee received a referral from the OCE regarding Representative Shelley Berkley.

On March 20, 2012, the Committee voted not to establish an Investigative Subcommittee with regard to the arrests of four Members — Al Green, James P. McGovern, James P. Moran, and John W. Olver — for crossing a police line during a protest outside of the Embassy of Sudan.

On April 2, 2012, the Committee received a referral from the OCE related to the alleged use of campaign or leadership PAC funds for personal use by Representative Robert Andrews.

On June 28, 2012, the Committee received a referral from the OCE related to allegations that Representative Michael G. Grimm improperly solicited or received prohibited campaign funds, used his official position to obtain campaign contributions, and filed false campaign finance reports.

On August 30, 2012, the Committee received a referral from the OCE related to allegations regarding Representative William Owens.

On August 30, 2012, the Committee received a referral from the OCE related to allegations regarding Representative Aaron Schock.

On August 30, 2012, the Committee received a referral from the OCE related to the alleged use of campaign funds for personal use by Representative Silvestre Reyes.

On November 15, 2012, the Committee voted not to establish an Investigative Subcommittee with regard to the arrest of Joy Henrichs, an employee of the House, for driving under the influence.

On December 19, 2012, the Committee voted not to establish an Investigative Subcommittee with regard a charge filed against Representative Tim Ryan, for public intoxication.

On December 19, 2012, the Committee completed its review of allegations related to the "V.I.P." program of the Countrywide Financial Corporation (Countrywide).

These investigative matters are described in more detail below.

Representatives John Campbell, Tom Price, and Joseph Crowley (In the Matter of Allegations Relating to Fundraising Activities and the House Vote on H.R. 4173)

On September 1, 2010, the OCE forwarded to the Committee a Report and Findings in which it recommended further review of allegations of campaign fundraising by Representatives John Campbell and Torn Price that was connected to a mark-up and vote on financial regulation legislation. As part of the same investigation, the OCE referred the matter of Representative Joseph Crowley. However, in accordance with H. Res. 895, and Committee Rule 17A(i), the OCE waited to make its referral of findings until November 3, 2010, after the primary and general elections.

In all three matters, the OCE alleged that the Members' fundraising activities near the time that the House voted on H.R. 4173 (Wall Street Reform and Consumer Protection Act of 2009) on December 11, 2009, gave the appearance that special treatment or access was provided to campaign donors, or gave the appearance that campaign contributions were linked to an official act.[1]

On December 15, 2010, pursuant to Committee Rules 17A(b)(1)(A) and 17A(j), the then-Chair and then-Ranking Republican Member jointly decided to extend the matter of Representatives Campbell, Price, and Crowley.

On January 26, 2011, the Chairman and Ranking Member of the Committee for the 112th Congress issued a public statement and released the. Report of the Committee's nonpartisan, professional staff. The Report concluded there was no violation of any House rule, or any law, rule, regulation or other standard of conduct by any of the three Members in relation to their fundraising and vote on the financial regulation legislation nor was there any appearance of impropriety.

The staff Report based its conclusions on the fact that each Member had employed a strict separation between all fundraising and legislative activities by hiring professional fundraising consultants to manage all aspects of fundraising events. These fundraising consultants had no interaction with the three Members or their legislative staff on legislative activities. The fundraising events were planned several months in advance, long before votes on the legislation at issue, and invitations to the fundraising events were not restricted to individuals associated with a particular industry. Each Member held consistent and well-established legislative positions regarding H.R. 4173 long before and after any of the fundraising events cited in the OCE's Reports and Findings. Each Member's official acts relating to H.R. 4173 were based on significant legislative concerns, which did not stem from requests from campaign donors. The record showed that the timing for floor action on H.R. 4173 was in constant flux, and was not known with certainty until days before the vote occurred on December 11, 2009.

Accordingly, the Committee's staff concluded that the general characteristics of each Member's fundraising events exhibited no appearances of special access for attendees to the Members in their official capacity and the Members did not violate any House rule, or any law, rule, regulation or other standard of conduct. In their January 26 statement, the Chairman and Ranking Member jointly announced that no further actions would be taken.

Representative Jean Schmidt[2]

On May 18, 2011, the OCE forwarded to the Committee a Report and Findings in which it recommended further review of allegations that Representative Jean Schmidt violated House Rules by accepting legal services from an outside entity without establishing a Legal Expense Fund and failing to report the legal services on her Financial Disclosure Statements for calendar years 2008 and 2009. The Committee conducted an investigation into the matter pursuant to Committee Rule 18(a).

On July 1, 2011, the Chairman and Ranking Member of the Committee jointly decided to extend the Committee's review of the OCE referral pursuant to House Rule XI, clause 3(a)(8)(A), and Committee Rules 17A(b)(1)(A) and 17A(c)(1).

On August 1, 2011, following the conclusion of the Committee's review, the Committee unanimously voted to release a public Report finding that Representative Schmidt did not knowingly violate any provision of the Code of Official Conduct or any law, rule, regulation, or other standard of conduct with respect to the receipt of gifts. The Committee released its Report and the OCE's Report and Findings on August 5, 2011.

The Committee's Report found that, beginning in spring of 2009, Representative Schmidt was involved in litigation regarding statements made about her by an opponent in her 2008 reelection campaign. That dispute involved proceedings before an Ohio state agency, in Ohio state court, and in federal court.

According to the OCE referral, Representative Schmidt received an impermissible gift from the Turkish Coalition of America (TCA) when lawyers provided legal services to Representative Schmidt in connection with the three matters and then sent bills for their fees to the TCA, which paid those bills on an ongoing basis.

According to the OCE's referral, between 2008 and 2010, TCA paid Representative Schmidt's lawyers, who claimed to be acting as the Turkish American Legal Defense Fund (TALDF), a project of TCA, approximately $500,000 for legal services provided to Representative Schmidt.

The Committee's review of the matter indicated that Representative Schmidt did, in fact, receive an impermissible gift from TCA as the OCE alleged, and therefore the Committee did not dismiss the OCE matter. However, the Committee found that Representative Schmidt's lawyers failed to inform her of their payment arrangement with TCA, and made false and misleading statements to her about their relationship with TCA and TALDF. Because Representative Schmidt did not know she was receiving a gift from TCA, the Committee determined that no sanction was appropriate in the case. However, the Committee concluded that the gift was impermissible, and thus required Representative Schmidt to disclose and repay the gift.

Through a letter to Representative Schmidt issued contemporaneously with the Committee's Report, the Committee directed Representative Schmidt to: (1) ensure that TCA did not pay for any further legal services on her behalf; (2) pay from a permissible source the lawyers associated with TALDF for all legal services they performed to date; (3) amend her 2009 and 2010 Financial Disclosure Statements to disclose the gifts from TCA; and (4) disclose any unpaid legal fees from TCA as liabilities on her future Financial Disclosure Statements, until the lawyers associated with TALDF have been repaid in full.

On August 16, 2011, after the Committee approved a request first submitted in 2009, Representative Schmidt established a Legal Expense Fund. On January 3, 2012, Representative Schmidt amended her 2009 and 2010 Financial Disclosure Statements. In August 2012, Representative Schmidt informed the Committee that she "had raised or personally paid approximately $50,000" to divest herself of the improper gift. Representative Schmidt lost her primary election and the Committee will not have jurisdiction over her after January 3, 2013.

Representative Gregory W. Meeks[3]

On May 18, 2011, the OCE forwarded to the Committee a Report and Findings in which it recommended further review of allegations that Representative Gregory W. Meeks failed to disclose a $40,000 loan he received from Edul Ahmad (Ahmad loan) and that the Ahmad loan was and should have been disclosed as a gift on Representative Meeks' Financial Disclosure Statements for 2007, 2008, and 2009.[4] On July 1, 2011, the Chairman and Ranking Member announced that they had jointly decided to extend the Committee's review of the matter for a 45-day period pursuant to Committee Rules 17A(b)(1)(A) and 17A(c).

On August 1, 2011, the Committee released the OCE's Report and Findings and indicated that it would continue to review allegations related to the Ahmad loan pursuant to Committee Rule 18(a).

Based on its investigation, the Committee adopted a Report on December 18, 2012, which resolves the allegation regarding the Ahmad loan. The Committee unanimously determined, based on the Committee's review of this allegation, that Representative Meeks failed to disclose the Ahmad loan as a liability on his 2007, 2008, and 2009 Financial Disclosure Statements. The Committee found no credible evidence that the errors were knowing or willful.

Although it was not the basis of the OCE referral, the Committee also investigated the allegation that the Ahmad loan was not accompanied by a written document and stated loan terms, and constituted an impermissible gift. The Committee determined that the evidence did not establish that the Ahmad loan was an impermissible gift.

Accordingly, on December 18, 2012 the Committee unanimously voted to adopt a Report concluding this matter. On December 20, 2012, the Committee transmitted its Report to the House of Representatives.

Michael Collin[5]

On May 18, 2011, the OCE forwarded to the Committee a Report and Findings in which it recommended further review of allegations that, in 2009, Michael Collins, an employee of the House, may have received outside income in excess of the outside earned income limit applicable to senior staff, and that Mr. Collins failed to report outside income on his annual Financial Disclosure Statements and federal income tax returns. On July 1, 2011, the Chairman and Ranking Member of the Committee jointly decided to extend the Committee's review of the OCE referral pursuant to House Rule XI, clause 3(a)(8)(A), and Committee Rules 17A(b)(1)(A) and 17A(c)(1).

The Committee conducted an investigation into the matter pursuant to Committee Rule 18(a). At the conclusion of its investigation, the Committee unanimously determined that Mr. Collins failed to report outside income he had earned from 2005 through 2010 on both his annual Financial Disclosure Statements and his federal income taxes for each year. The Committee also found that, in 2009, Mr. Collins received an excess of $450 of outside earned income that he repaid in 2011 in order to disgorge himself of the excess outside earned income. Mr. Collins agreed to waive all further procedural steps and rights he may have been entitled to under House and Committee Rules and to accept certain sanctions and remedies. Mr. Collins agreed to accept the findings of the Committee, accept a Letter of Reproval from the Committee for his actions, pay a $1,000 fine, amend his Financial Disclosure Statements and federal income tax returns for 2005 through 2010, and pay any taxes or penalties owed. Accordingly, on August 1, 2011, the Committee unanimously voted to adopt a Report concluding this matter. On August 5, 2011, the Committee transmitted its Report to the House of Representatives.

Gregory Hill[6]

On May 18, 2011, the OCE forwarded to the Committee a Report and Findings in which it recommended further review of allegations that, in 2009, Gregory Hill, an employee of the House, may have received outside income in excess of the outside earned income limit applicable to senior staff, and that Mr. Hill failed to properly report the actual amount of such income on his 2009 Financial Disclosure Statement. On July 1, 2011, the Chairman and Ranking Member of the Committee jointly decided to extend the Committee's review of the OCE referral pursuant to House Rule XI, clause 3(a)(8)(A), and Committee Rules 17A(b)(1)(A) and 17A(c)(1).

The Committee conducted an investigation into the matter pursuant to Committee Rule 18(a). At the conclusion of its investigation, the Committee unanimously determined that, in 2009, Mr. Hill did in fact receive outside income that exceeded the outside earned income limit for senior staff However, the Committee determined that Mr. Hill had taken several steps to ensure that his outside income remained within the authorized amount for senior staff. In addition, the Committee found that Mr. Hill's outside employer was responsible for the clerical error which led to Mr. Hill's receipt of outside income that exceeded the limit for senior staff Further, the Committee determined that when Mr. Hill learned of the error, he took corrective action and repaid the excess amount. Finally, while Mr. Hill did not report the amount actually received in 2009 on his 2009 Financial Disclosure Statement, the Committee found that he relied upon information provided by the outside employer, including official wage and earnings statements to complete his Financial Disclosure Statement and that the information supplied to him was incorrect without his knowledge. The Committee found that because Mr. Hill had repaid the excess amount, making the total received for 2009 below the limit, no further action was necessary. Accordingly, on August 1, 2011, the Committee unanimously voted to adopt a Report concluding this matter. On August 5, 2011, the Committee transmitted its Report to the House of Representatives.

Matters Related to Allegations Against Former Representative Eric Massa

On July 14, 2011, the Committee voted to re-authorize an Investigative Subcommittee for the 112th Congress that had been previously authorized during the 111th Congress for the matter involving former Representative Eric Massa. The Investigative Subcommittee was again charged with conducting a full and complete inquiry into whether any Member, officer, or employee, in the performance of the duties or the discharge of the responsibilities of such individual: (1) had personal knowledge of actual or alleged conduct by Representative Massa that violated a law, rule, regulation, or other standard of conduct applicable to his conduct in the performance of his duties; (2) failed properly to report or fully disclose any such actual or alleged conduct on the part of Representative Massa; (3) had a duty to pursue or call attention to such allegations of misconduct; or (4) misappropriated, or otherwise fraudulently or improperly distributed or received, monies or other payments, all of the foregoing in violation of any law, rule, regulation or other standard of conduct.

Each of the Members who had initially served on the Investigative Subcommittee in the 111th Congress was reappointed in the 112th Congress. Representative Jo Bonner, the Chairman of the Committee on Ethics, served as Chairman of the Investigative Subcommittee. Representative Zoe Lofgren served as the Ranking Member. The other two members of the subcommittee were Representative Michael Conaway and Representative Ben Chandler.

As of the conclusion of the 112th Congress, the Investigative Subcommittee had not completed its investigation into the matter under its jurisdiction.

Representative Maxine Waters?

On July 24, 2009, the OCE forwarded to the Committee a Report and Findings in which it recommended further review of allegations that Representative Maxine Waters violated House Rule XXIII, clause 3 and House precedent regarding conflicts of interest when she called the then-Treasury Secretary and requested that Treasury Department officials meet with representatives from the National Bankers Association. The OCE alleged that this meeting focused on a single bank—OneUnited Bank (OneUnited)—in which Representative Waters' husband held stock and for which he had previously served on the Board of Directors.

On October 29, 2009, following an investigation by Committee staff pursuant to authority granted by the Chairman and Ranking Member under Committee Rule 18(a), the Committee established an Investigative Subcommittee (ISC). During the course of the investigation, the ISC (in the 111th Congress) issued 11 subpoenas, interviewed 13 witnesses, and reviewed more than 1,300 pages of documents.

In the spring of 2010, the ISC came to an agreement to release a Report critical of some conduct in the matter, but recommending no further action or sanction. However, the former Chief Counsel and Staff Director advised the Committee that the rules did not permit an ISC to issue a Report that was critical of a Member without adopting a Statement of Alleged Violation (SAV) and providing the Respondent with the opportunity for an adjudicatory hearing under the rules for an Adjudicatory Subcommittee.

Subsequently, on June 15, 2010, the ISC adopted an SAV alleging three counts of misconduct: violations of clauses 1 and 3 of the House Code of Official Conduct (House Rule XXIII), and paragraph 5 of the Code of Ethics for Government Service. The ISC transmitted the SAV to the full Committee on July 28, 2010. Shortly thereafter, the Committee established an Adjudicatory Subcommittee (ASC) to conduct a hearing on the SAV.

On October 7, 2010, the Chair of the ASC scheduled a hearing in Representative Waters' matter for November 21, 2010. On or about October 12, 2010, the Committee postponed the date of the hearing by one week, until November 29, 2010.

On November 15, 2010, two weeks before the hearing was to occur, staff submitted a formal motion to the ASC to recommit the matter to the ISC, on the grounds that staff had obtained new evidence in the matter. On November 18, 2010, the ASC voted to recommit the matter to the ISC.

By the end of the 111th Congress, the Committee recognized the need to hire Outside Counsel to complete this matter. However, the need to reconstitute the Connnittee's staff in the 112th Congress delayed the resolution of Representative Waters' matter by, among other things, delaying the retention of Outside Counsel. The Committee ultimately retained attorney Billy Martin to serve as Outside Counsel on July 20, 2011.

The Committee's first charge to Outside Counsel was a thorough review of serious allegations regarding the Committee's own conduct in this matter. Those allegations included charges that the Committee and its staff had violated Representative Waters' due process rights in several respects during the course of the Committee's investigation. Mr. Martin thus conducted an extensive review of allegations raised by both Representative Waters and the Committee itself, which included a document review comprising more than 100,000 pages, interviews of 26 witnesses, including all Members of the Committee from the 111th Congress as well as all current and former staff with knowledge of the relevant issues, and a significant and thorough analysis of the relevant legal issues. The vast majority of this review took place between July 2011 and the end of 2011. However, one significant witness, refused to testify without the issuance of a subpoena, and then indicated an intention to assert the Fifth Amendment privilege when the subpoena was issued. The witness did ultimately provide testimony, but the witness's recalcitrance delayed the completion of the first phase of Outside Counsel's review by at least four months.

On February 17, 2012, based on the advice received from Outside Counsel, six Members of the Committee for the 112th Congress—the

Chairman, the Ranking Member, and all current Committee Members who also served on the Committee during the 111th Congress—voluntarily requested recusal from this matter. Further, all current Committee staff who were involved in Representative Waters' matter in the 111th Congress were recused from the matter.

Outside Counsel did not find any evidence of wrongdoing by any Member of the Committee, and no Member requested recusal because of any such wrongdoing. Instead, the Members requested recusal because:

1. They believed that, out of an abundance of caution and to avoid even an appearance of unfairness, their voluntary recusal would eliminate the possibility of questions being raised as to the partiality or bias of Committee Members considering this matter;
2. They wanted to assure the public, the House, and Representative Waters that this investigation was continuing in a fair and unbiased manner; and
3. They wanted to move this matter forward in a manner that supported the greatest public confidence in the ultimate conclusions of this Committee.

On February 17, 2012, the Speaker of the House of Representatives, with input from the Minority Leader, appointed six substitute Committee members who were charged solely with resolving Representative Waters' matter. The six new Committee members, Representatives Bob Goodlatte, Mike Simpson, Steve LaTourette, Shelley Moore Capito, Tim Griffin, and John Sarbanes, joined the four members of the standing Committee who had no role in the investigation of Representative Waters' matter in the 111th Congress. These 10 Members were referred to as the "Waters Committee." Representative Goodlatte served as the acting Chairman and Representative John Yannuth, of the standing Committee, served as the acting Ranking Member.

Upon completion of Outside Counsel's due process review, Outside Counsel submitted his conclusions from that review to the Waters Committee in May 2012. On June 6, 2012, the Acting Chairman and Acting Ranking Member of the Waters Committee wrote to Representative Waters, notifying her that upon the advice of Outside Counsel, the Waters Committee had unanimously found that none of the individual allegations raised regarding the conduct of Committee Members or staff, nor the totality of the circumstances of those claims, amounted to a deprivation of her due process rights.

Only upon conclusion of the first phase of the review was Outside Counsel authorized to conduct a *de novo* review of the actual substance of the allegations against Representative Waters. This review was similarly thorough; Outside Counsel reviewed all prior ISC and staff interview transcripts and all documents produced to the Committee, and also re-interviewed several key witnesses. Members of the Waters Committee also reviewed many of these ISC and staff interview transcripts and key documents. Finally, after providing Representative Waters and her chief of staff the opportunity to appear before the Committee, the Waters Committee held a public hearing on September 21, 2012. The Committee heard Representative Waters' chief of staff's testimony and fully considered it.

Based on the work of Outside Counsel, the Waters Committee's own evaluation of that work, and Representative Waters' chief of staff's testimony at the public hearing, the Waters Committee made their own determinations with respect to Representative Waters and her chief of staff.

With respect to Representative Waters' actions to set up a meeting between the then-Treasury Secretary and representatives from the National Bankers Association—who were also associated with OneUnited—Outside Counsel concluded that Representative Waters reasonably believed, at the time she requested the meeting, that the attendees would be speaking on behalf of minority banks generally. While it appears that all of the minority bankers who attended the meeting were associated with OneUnited, and that OneUnited was alone in requesting substantial financial assistance from the Treasury Department at the meeting, the record indicates that Representative Waters did not have reason to know of either of these facts when she arranged the meeting. Accordingly, Outside Counsel recommended that the Waters Committee find that Representative Waters reasonably believed she was arranging the Treasury meeting on behalf of a broad class of minority banks, and that in doing so she did not violate any House rule, law, regulation, or other applicable standard of conduct. The Waters Committee unanimously agreed with Outside Counsel's recommendation.

Outside Counsel also reviewed allegations that Representative Waters' chief of staff took steps to assist OneUnited after Representative Waters realized that the bank made a request for federal financial assistance from the Treasury Department and that, due to her significant financial interest in OneUnited, she had a conflict of interest regarding any efforts to provide specific financial assistance to OneUnited. Outside Counsel concurred in Representative Waters' determination that she had a conflict of interest with respect to OneUnited's request for specific financial assistance. Outside

Counsel also recognized that the House Rules prohibit Members from doing anything through staff that the Rules prohibit them from doing directly. Further, longstanding Committee precedent holds Members responsible for the actions of their staff, when those actions are within the scope of the staffs official duties. Thus, Outside Counsel believed that if Representative Waters' chief of staff knowingly ignored Representative Waters' conflict of interest—after the conflict became clear—and facilitated OneUnited's request for federal financial assistance, Representative Waters could be responsible for violating House rules.

However, Outside Counsel recommended that the Committee find that the evidence did not establish that Representative Waters violated House Rules. As Outside Counsel's Report detailed, Representative Waters appeared to have recognized and made efforts to avoid a conflict of interest with respect to OneUnited. Accordingly, Outside Counsel recommended that the Waters Committee find that Representative Waters did not violate House Rules by failing to exercise adequate oversight of her chief of staff with respect to his work on behalf of OneUnited. The Waters Committee unanimously concurred with this conclusion.

Outside Counsel also analyzed the conduct of Representative Waters' chief of staff, who is also her grandson. Outside Counsel considered evidence that Representative Waters told her chief of staff of her conflict of interest with respect to OneUnited prior to September 19, 2008, the date on which the chief of staff sent the first of two emails that were unambiguously intended to assist OneUnited specifically. Although Outside Counsel concluded that the evidence did not establish, to a clear and convincing level, that Representative Waters' chief of staff was directed not to work on OneUnited matters before September 19, 2008, Outside Counsel believed that there was evidence to support that finding, and informed the Waters Committee that, based on its own weighing of the evidence, the Waters Committee could reasonably make that determination.

Outside Counsel also considered evidence, including Representative Waters' own testimony, that suggested that Representative Waters' chief of staff knew or should have known—regardless of how and when Representative Waters instructed her chief of staff not to work on OneUnited matters—that Representative Waters had a significant financial interest in, and thus a potential conflict of interest with respect to, OneUnited. Outside Counsel recognized this evidence, but recommended that the record, standing alone, did not establish the conclusion to a clear and convincing standard. Outside Counsel thus deferred to the Waters Committee to weigh the credibility of the chief of staff's claimed ignorance of Representative Waters' financial interest in OneUnited, in light of the evidence to the contrary. The Waters Committee ultimately found that the totality of the evidence supported the conclusion that the chief of staff knew or should have known of Representative Waters' financial interest in OneUnited. Thus, the Waters Committee found that the chief of staff knew or should have known that Representative Waters had a conflict of interest with respect to specific actions to assist OneUnited, regardless of how and when Representative Waters informed him that she believed such a conflict existed.

Based on the foregoing findings, the Waters Committee voted unanimously to close its investigation regarding Representative Waters. However, the Waters Committee found that Representative Waters' chief of staff knew or should have known of Representative Waters' financial interest in OneUnited and her conflict of interest in taking official action on the bank's behalf alone, and that the chief of staff thus violated House rules by taking specific actions that would accrue to the distinct benefit of OneUnited. Accordingly, the Committee unanimously voted to issue a Letter of Reproval to Representative Waters' chief of staff for his conduct. On September 25, 2012, the Waters Committee issued its Report in the matter of Representative Waters, which included the final Report of Outside Counsel.

Representative Luis V. Gutierrez[8]

In accordance with the requirements of H. Res. 451, H. Res. 5, Section 4(d) and Committee Rule 18(e)(2), the Committee convened on August 1, 2011, to consider the arrest of Representative Luis V. Gutierrez for failure to obey a lawful order from a police officer during a protest outside the White House on July 26, 2011. Representative Gutierrez paid a $100 fine and was released following his arrest. Payment of the fine ended legal proceedings in the District of Columbia with regard to the arrest.

After reviewing and considering this matter, the Committee voted against empanelling an Investigative Subcommittee related to the conduct of Representative Gutierrez. In reaching this decision, the Committee considered the scope and nature of the violation, and determined it to be one for which review by an Investigative Subcommittee was not required. On August 5, 2011, the Committee submitted a Report to the House of Representatives describing the facts and its findings regarding this matter.

Representative Jesse Jackson, Jr.

On August 6, 2009, the OCE referred to the Committee allegations regarding Representative Jesse Jackson, Jr. Pursuant to a request by the Department of Justice, the Committee voted on September 15, 2009, to defer investigation of the matter. On October 13, 2011, the Department informed the Committee that it would not request any further deferral of the Committee's investigation regarding Representative Jackson. The Committee then voted to end the deferral period on October 13, 2011. On October 18, 2011, the Chairman and Ranking Member jointly decided to extend the matter of Representative Jackson for a 45-day period pursuant to Committee Rules 17A(b)(1)(A) and 17A(c)(1). On December 2, 2011, the Chairman and Ranking Member released a public statement that, pursuant to Committee Rule 18(a), the Committee would continue to review the matter. On that same date, pursuant to Committee Rule 17A(c)(2), the Committee published OCE's Report and Findings relating to allegations against Representative Jackson.

Representative Jackson resigned from the House on November 21, 2012, and the Committee no longer has jurisdiction over him. As of that date the Committee had not completed its investigation into this matter.

Todd Poole[9]

In accordance with the requirements of Committee Rule 18(e)(2), the Committee convened on September 8, 2011, to consider the arrest of Todd Poole, an employee of the House, on August 11, 2011, in North Carolina for driving while impaired and resisting an officer. After reviewing and considering this matter, the Committee voted against empanelling an Investigative Subcommittee. In reaching this decision, the Committee considered the scope and nature of the violation, and determined it to be one for which review by an Investigative Subcommittee was not required. On September 9, 2011, the Committee submitted a Report to the House of Representatives describing the facts and its findings regarding this matter.

Representative Don Young[10]

June 23, 2011, the OCE commenced a preliminary review of allegations that Representative Don Young had accepted contributions to his Legal

Expense Fund (LEF) in excess of the limits established by applicable rules. Pursuant to its organizing resolution, the OCE was required to notify both Representative Young and the Committee that it had begun a preliminary review. In a letter dated July 6, 2011, Representative Young sought guidance from the Committee related to twelve $5,000 contributions—the maximum contribution permitted—made to his LEF by twelve limited liability corporations (LLCs) located in Louisiana. Representative Young indicated that, prior to accepting the contributions, his office sought guidance from the LEF's trustee, Gail R. Schubert, regarding whether contributions from companies that are separate legal entities and "operate under separate financial records" were subject to the same contribution limit. The trustee's opinion was that such contributions were permissible and not subject to the same contribution limit if the companies were separate legal entities and operated under separate financial records.

On October 13, 2011, the OCE forwarded to the Committee a Report and Findings in which it recommended further review of allegations that Representative Young may have accepted contributions to his LEF in excess of the $5,000 per calendar year limit from any individual or organization.

On November 17, 2011, the Chairman and Ranking Member authorized an investigation pursuant to Committee Rule 18(a) to gather additional information related to the allegations in the OCE's Report and Findings. The Committee also conducted a review of the advice generally given to individuals with LEFs in interpreting the Legal Expense Fund Regulations issued by the Committee on June 10, 1996 (1996 LEF Regulations). Based on the information gathered during the 18(a) investigation, as well as the Committee's review of the advice generally given, on December 14, 2011, the Committee voted unanimously to resolve the issues surrounding Representative Young's outstanding request for guidance from the Committee and the allegations referred by the OCE, by issuing a letter to Representative Young and releasing a Report.

With respect to Representative Young's request for guidance from the Committee, the Committee, in guidance issued contemporaneously with the Report on December 20, 2011, determined that the $5,000 contributions by the twelve Louisiana LLCs to Representative Young were permissible under the 1996 LEF Regulations issued by the Committee, and that the LEF's acceptance of those contributions did not violate House rules. The Committee also adopted revised LEF Regulations, issued contemporaneously with the Report, that provide clarity on several matters related to LEFs, including restrictions on contributions from multiple entities owned by the same individual or individuals.

The Committee also dismissed the allegations in the OCE referral. With respect to the referral from OCE, the Committee determined that, based on the 1996 LEF Regulations and long-standing Committee advice, multiple entities owned by the same individual or individuals were permitted to make contributions up to $5,000 per entity if they were separate legal entities. The twelve Louisiana LLCs were separate legal entities and were separately registered with the Louisiana Secretary of State. Further, the entities provide separate and distinct products or services and were formed at different times. Based on those reasons, the Committee voted to dismiss OCE' s referral.

Representative Alcee L. Hastings

On November 8, 2011, the OCE forwarded to the Committee a Report and Findings in which it recommended further review of allegations that Representative Alcee L. Hastings may have violated House Rule XXIII, clause 1, and the Congressional Accountability Act, 2 U.S.C. §§ 1311(a), 1317(a), where he allegedly engaged in employment discrimination, unwelcome sexual advances, and unwelcome sexual conduct towards a staffer of the United States Commission on Security and Cooperation in Europe. The Committee released OCE's Report and Findings on January 11, 2012, and noted in a public statement that the Committee was continuing to review the allegations pursuant to Committee Rule 18(a).

As of the conclusion of the 112th Congress the Committee had not completed its investigation into this matter.

Representative Laura Richardson[11]

In October 2010, the Committee received complaints from several members of Representative Laura Richardson's staff in both her Washington, D.C., and Long Beach, California, offices, indicating that Representative Richardson required her staff to perfonn campaign work. Based on these complaints, the then-Chair and then-Ranking Republican Member of the Committee for the 111th Congress authorized Committee staff to conduct an inquiry into these allegations pursuant to Committee Rule 18(a). On October 15, 2010, Committee counsel notified Representative Richardson in writing of the inquiry and requested she make her staff and documents and records available to the Committee. During the 18(a) phase of the inquiry, Committee staff obtained documents from Representative Richardson and her staff and interviewed 17 witnesses, including members of Representative Richardson's staff.

On November 3, 2011, based on the results of the 18(a) investigation and the recommendation of Committee staff, the Committee empanelled an Investigative Subcommittee (ISC) to investigate allegations that Representative Richardson, as well as two members of her official staff, had (1) engaged in improper use of House resources for campaign, personal, and nonofficial purposes; and (2) improperly required or compelled official staff to perform campaign work.

At the completion of its investigation, the ISC unanimously concluded that there was substantial reason to believe that Representative Richardson had violated 31 U.S.C. § 1301; House Rule XXIII clauses 1, 2, and 8; clause 2 of the Code of Ethics for Government Service; and other standards of conduct, by improperly using House resources for campaign, personal, and nonofficial purposes; by requiring or compelling her official staff to perform campaign work; and by obstructing the investigation of the Committee and the ISC through the alteration or destruction of evidence, the deliberate failure to produce documents responsive to requests for information and a subpoena, and/or attempting to influence the testimony of witnesses.

On July 18, 2012, pursuant to a negotiated settlement with Representative Richardson, the ISC unanimously voted to adopt a Statement of Alleged Violation (SAV) against Representative Richardson. On July 26, 2012, the ISC submitted a Report to the full Committee unanimously recommending that the full Committee submit a public report to the House. The ISC further recommended that the adoption of that Report by the House would serve as a reprimand of Representative Richardson for her misconduct. Additionally, the ISC recommended that the Committee recommend that the House impose a fine on Representative Richardson in the amount of $10,000, to be paid no later than December 1, 2012. The ISC strongly discouraged Representative Richardson from permitting any of her official staff to perfonn work on her campaign (either on a paid or volunteer basis), but recommended to the Committee that, to the extent any of her official staff did perform work on her campaign in the future, that said staff be required to sign a waiver asserting that such work would be performed voluntarily and was not compelled by Representative Richardson. As part of the negotiated resolution, Representative Richardson agreed to waive all further procedural rights in the matter provided to her by House or Committee rules, and agreed to admit to all seven counts in the SAV, pay a $10,000 fine by December 1, 2012, and accept all other terms of the ISC's recommendation.

As part of its investigation, the ISC also inquired as to the role of Representative Richardson's Chief of Staff, Shirley Cooks, and Deputy District Director, Daysha Austin, in this matter. Following its investigation, the ISC concluded that Ms. Cooks and Ms. Austin had required other members of Representative Richardson's staff to perform campaign work and had used House resources for campaign purposes. Pursuant to separate negotiated settlements, Ms. Cooks and Ms. Austin each agreed to waive all further procedural rights in the matter provided to them by House or Committee rules. The ISC then recommended that the Committee issue public letters of reproval to Ms. Cooks and Ms. Austin for their conduct. The Committee accepted this recommendation and issued public Letters of Reproval to Ms. Cooks and Ms. Austin on August 1, 2012.

On August 1, 2012, the Committee submitted to the House its Report regarding this matter, in which the Committee adopted the ISC's Report and all of its recommendations. Following debate before the full House, the House of Representatives adopted the Committee's Report regarding Representative Richardson by unanimous consent on August 2, 2012, and thus reprimanded her for her use of official resources for campaign and personal purposes, and for obstruction of the Committee's investigation. By adopting the Committee's Report, the House of Representatives also imposed a $10,000 fine on Representative Richardson, as recommended by the ISC and full Committee.

Representative Vern Buchanan (Financial Disclosure Statements)[12]

On November 8, 2011, the OCE forwarded to the Committee a Report and Findings in which it recommended further review of allegations that Representative Vern Buchanan may have violated House Rule XXVI, clause 2, and the Ethics in Government Act, 5 U.S.C. app. 4 § 101 *et seq.*, by failing to properly list on his Financial Disclosure Statements for 2007 through 2010 certain positions with a number of entities, as well as certain income from those positions. Representative Buchanan amended his 2007 through 2010 Financial Disclosure Statements while the OCE conducted its investigation. On February 6, 2012, pursuant to Committee Rule 17A(c)(2), the Committee published the OCE's Report and Findings relating to allegations against Representative Buchanan.

After conducting an investigation of this matter pursuant to Committee Rule 18(a), the Committee issued a Report on July 10, 2012, in which it unanimously concluded that Representative Buchanan did not report on his Financial Disclosure Statements for 2007, 2008, 2009, and 2010, in complete and accurate detail, all of the positions or ownership interests he held with several entities and that he did not accurately report certain income received from those same entities in the same years. However, the Committee also unanimously determined that these errors and omissions were not substantively different from the hundreds or thousands of errors and omissions corrected by amendment at the requirement of the Committee every year. Because Representative Buchanan had remedied the errors and omissions by his subsequent amendments, the Committee determined that no further action was warranted in this matter.

Representative Vern Buchanan (Campaign Finance/Witness Tampering)

On February 9, 2012, the OCE forwarded to the Committee a Report and Findings in which it recommended further review of allegations that Representative Vern Buchanan may have violated 18 U.S.C. §§ 201, 1505, and 1512, as well as House Rule XXIII, clause 1, by making the settlement of a lawsuit against a former business partner contingent on the business partner signing a false affidavit to be filed with the Federal Election Commission. The Committee released the OCE's Report and Findings on May 9, 2012, and noted in a public statement that the Committee was continuing to review the allegations pursuant to Committee Rule 18(a).

As of the conclusion of the 112th Congress the Committee had not completed its investigation into this matter.

Representative Shelley Berkley[13]

On February 9, 2012, the OCE forwarded to the Committee a Report and Findings in which it recommended further review of allegations that Representative Shelley Berkley used her official position for personal gain and violated conflict of interest precedent by taking official action on behalf of the

University Medical Center of Southern Nevada (UMC) Kidney Transplant Program in order to prevent the Centers for Medicare and Medicaid Services (CMS) from terminating the program's Medicare approval. On March 23, 2012, the Chairman and Ranking Member issued a public statement and jointly extended the matter referred by the OCE for an additional 45 days. Prior to the end of the second 45-day period, on June 29, 2012, the full Committee voted unanimously to empanel an Investigative Subcommittee to investigate allegations that Representative Shelley Berkley improperly used her official position for her financial interest, dispensed special favors or privileges to her husband, and allowed her husband to contact her or members of her staff on behalf of a third party.

The ISC unanimously concluded that the information it obtained indicated that Representative Berkley violated House Rules, regulations, laws or other standards of conduct when she permitted her office to take official action specifically on behalf of her husband's practice. However, the ISC did not find that Representative Berkley violated any such rules or laws when she intervened on behalf of UMC in an effort to prevent CMS from terminating Medicare approval of UMC's kidney transplant program, or when she permitted her husband to contact her office on behalf of other business entities, fellow members of a professional association, or other third parties seeking official action. The ISC adopted its Report on December 13, 2012, and transmitted it to the full Committee on the same day. In its Report, the ISC noted that Representative Berkley was entirely cooperative with the investigation, and credited her testimony both in terms of candor, and in terms of her objective lack of malicious intent in violating the rules.

On December 20, 2012, after providing Representative Berkley with a copy of the ISC' s Report and inviting her to a hearing before the full Committee, the Committee unanimously adopted its own Report. In its Report, the Committee adopted the ISC' s Report and accepted the ISC' s recommendations. On December 20, 2012, the Committee submitted its Report to the House and closed this matter.

In the Matter of the Sudanese Embassy Protest Arrests[14]

In accordance with the requirements of H. Res. 451, H. Res. 5, Section 4(d) and Committee Rule 18(e)(2), the Committee convened on March 20, 2012, to consider the arrests of four Members— Representatives Al Green, James P. McGovern, James P. Moran, and John W. Olver— for crossing a police line during a protest outside the Embassy of Sudan on March 16, 2012. Each of the four Members paid a $100 fine on the date of their arrest. Payment of the fine ended legal proceedings in the District of Columbia with regard to each arrest.

After reviewing and considering this matter, the Committee voted against empanelling an Investigative Subcommittee. In reaching this decision, the Committee considered the scope and nature of the violation, and determined it to be one for which review by an Investigative Subcommittee was not required. On March 22, 2012, the Committee submitted a Report to the House of Representatives describing the facts and its findings regarding this matter.

Representative Robert E. Andrews

On April 2, 2012, the OCE forwarded to the Committee a Report and Findings in which it recommended further review of allegations that Representative Robert Andrews converted funds from his principal campaign committee and leadership political action committee (PAC) to personal use by paying for trips to Scotland and to California with family members from campaign and leadership PAC funds. Committee Rule 17A(j) provides that the Committee may postpone any reporting requirement related to an OCE referral that falls within that 60-day period until after the date of the election in which the subject of the referral is a candidate. Representative Andrews was on the primary ballot in June 2012. Therefore, the announcement that the Chairman and Ranking Member jointly decided to extend the matter of Representative Andrews for a 45-day period pursuant to Committee Rules 17A(b)(1)(A) and 17A(j) was postponed until July 17, 2012. On August 31, 2012, the Chairman and Ranking Member released a public statement that, pursuant to Committee Rule 18(a), the Committee would continue to review the matter. On that same date, pursuant to Committee Rule 17A(c)(2), the Committee published OCE's Report and Findings relating to allegations against Representative Andrews.

As of the conclusion of the 112th Congress, the Committee had not completed its investigation into this matter.

Representative Michael G. Grimm

On June 29, 2012, the OCE forwarded to the Committee a Report in which it recommended dismissal of allegations that Representative Michael G.

Grimm violated federal campaign finance laws, where he allegedly solicited and accepted prohibited campaign contributions, including contributions in excess of contribution limits, excessive cash contributions, contributions from foreign nationals, and contributions made in the name of another. The OCE's Report contained additional allegations that Representative Grimm had filed false information in his campaign finance reports to the Federal Election Commission, and that he may have improperly sought assistance from a foreign national in soliciting campaign contributions in exchange for offering to use his official position to assist that individual in obtaining a green card. The OCE recommended dismissal because it "could not establish with sufficient certainty that a violation occurred after Representative Grimm became a Member of Congress."

On November 15, 2012, the Committee unanimously voted to continue to affirm jurisdiction over matters relating to a successful campaign for election to the House of Representatives. The Committee had previously taken this position with respect to its jurisdiction in other matters similar to these allegations, where Members had allegedly violated laws, rules, or standards of conduct when conducting their initial campaign for the House.[15] Because the Committee disagreed with the OCE's conclusion regarding its jurisdiction, the Committee decided to investigate the matter pursuant to Committee Rule 18(a). However, just before the Committee would have been required to issue the report of the OCE, the Department of Justice requested that the Committee defer its consideration of this matter. The Committee agreed to do so and, consistent with House and Committee Rules, publicly announced the deferral on November 26, 2012.

As of the conclusion of the 112th Congress the Committee had not completed its investigation into this matter.

Representative William L. Owens

On August 30, 2012, the OCE referred to the Committee allegations regarding Representative William L. Owens. On December 14, 2012, the Chairman and Ranking Member jointly decided to extend the matter of Representative William Owens for a 45-day period pursuant to Committee Rules 17A(b)(1)(A) and 17A(j).

Representative Aaron Schock

On August 30, 2012, the OCE referred to the Committee allegations regarding Representative Aaron Schock. On December 14, 2012, the Chairman and Ranking Member jointly decided to extend the matter of Representative Aaron Schock for a 45-day period pursuant to Committee Rules 17A(b)(1)(A) and 17A(j).

Representative Silvestre Reyes

On August 30, 2012, the OCE forwarded to the Committee a Report and Findings in which it recommended further review of allegations that Representative Silvestre Reyes violated 31 U.S.C. § 1301, 18 U.S.C. § 607, 2 U.S.C. § 439a(b)(1), 11 C.F.R. § 113.1(g)(1)(i)(E), and House Rule XXIII, clause 6(b), where public records indicated that Representative Reyes may have held campaign meetings on House property, and that he may have improperly used campaign funds to pay for certain expenses related to his daughter's residence. The Committee released OCE' s Report and Findings on November 28, 2012.

As of the conclusion of the 112th Congress, the Committee had not completed its investigation in this matter. Representative Reyes lost his primary election and the Committee will not have jurisdiction over him after January 3, 2013.

Joy Henrichs[16]

In accordance with the requirements of Committee Rule 18(e)(2), the Committee convened on November 15, 2012, to consider the arrest of Joy Henrichs, an employee of the House, on August 16, 2012, in Virginia for driving under the influence. After reviewing and considering this matter, the Committee voted against empanelling an Investigative Subcommittee. In reaching this decision, the Committee considered the scope and nature of the violation, and determined it to be one for which review by an Investigative Subcommittee was not required. On November 16, 2012, the Committee submitted a Report to the House of Representatives describing the facts and its findings regarding this matter.

Representative Tim Ryan[17]

In accordance with the requirements of H. Res. 451, H. Res. 5, Section 4(d) and Committee Rule 18(e)(2), the Committee convened on December 19, 2012, to consider the charge filed against Representative Tim Ryan on August 25, 2012, in Virginia for public intoxication. On December 4, 2012, Representative Ryan was found not guilty of the charge. After reviewing and considering this matter, the Committee voted against empanelling an investigative subcommittee. In reaching this decision, the Committee considered the scope and nature of the violation, and determined it to be one for which review by an investigative subcommittee was not required. On December 20, 2012, the Committee submitted a report to the House of Representatives describing the facts and its findings regarding this matter.

Countrywide Financial Corporation

On December 19, 2012, the Committee completed its review of allegations related to the "V.I.P." program of the Countrywide Financial Corporation (Countrywide). On December 27, 2012, the Chairman and Ranking Member issued a public statement regarding the resolution of this matter as well as a general advisory to Members and employees regarding the use of one's position in the House of Representatives for personal gain or benefit.

Numerous allegations were made that certain Members and employees of the House of Representatives acted improperly when they received "discounts" on personal residential or vacation property loans, or when their loan applications were handled by an office within Countrywide called the "V.I.P Loan Unit," or handled as "Friends of Angelo," referring to Angelo Mozilo, the former CEO of Countrywide. In addition, the evidence suggested that certain House employees made explicit requests to Countrywide lobbyists or spoke to a Countrywide lobbyist about their personal loan needs, and that the lobbyists then facilitated those loans.

While these allegations concern serious matters, almost all of the allegations concerned actions taken outside, or well outside, the jurisdiction of this Committee, as designated in House Rule XI, clause 3(b)(3), because they occurred before the third Congress prior to the current Congress. In addition, several of the Members and employees mentioned in the allegations are no longer serving in or employed by the House, and therefore are outside the Committee's jurisdiction pursuant to House Rule XI, clause 3(a)(2).

After a lengthy and deliberate review, including more than 2,000 of pages of documentation provided by Countrywide or its successor, Bank of America, as well as giving careful and serious consideration to the submission and reports of the Chairman of the Committee on Oversight and Government Reform, the Committee unanimously agreed to end its review with the publication of a statement and the issuance of a general advisory. That general advisory is available on the Committee's web site.

Other Committee Investigative Actions

In addition to the publicly disclosed matters discussed in this Report, the Committee either commenced review of, or continued to review from the 111th Congress, 69 investigative matters. Of these 69 matters which remain confidential, 42 were resolved in the 112th Congress.

Additional appendices to this report can be found online at: http://ethics.house.gov/committee-report/activities-committee-ethics-112th-congress.

End Notes

[1] As part of the same investigation, the OCE also recommended for dismissal the matters of Representatives Jeb Hensarling, Christopher Lee, Frank Lucas and Melvin L. Watt. The Committee took no further action in those matters.

[2] Committee on Ethics, *in the Matter of Allegations Relating to Representative Jean Schmidt,* H. Rept. 112-195, 112th Cong. 1st Sess. (2011).

[3] Committee on Ethics, *In the Matter of Allegations Relating to Representative Gregory Meeks,* H. Rept. 112-709, 112th Cong. 2d Sess. (2012).

[4] In the same Report and Findings, the OCE referred for dismissal allegations that Representative Meeks accepted an improper loan from a private investment firm (investment frm loan). The OCE based its dismissal recommendation on its conclusion that the investment firm loan had all the "normal indicia of a legitimate loan," and was thus not an improper gift that would violate the House gift rule. On August 1, 2011, the Committee voted unanimously to dismiss the allegation regarding the investment firm loan based on the evidence that the loan was commercially reasonable.

[5] Committee on Ethics, *In the Matter of Allegations Relating to Michael Collins,* H. Rept. 112-193, 112th Cong. 1st Sess. (2011).

[6] Committee on Ethics, *In the Matter of Allegations Relating to Gregory Hill,* H. Rept. 112-194, 112th Cong. 1st Sess. (2011).

[7] Committee on Ethics, *In the Matter of Representative Maxine Waters,* H. Rept. 112-690, 112th Cong. 2d Sess. (2012).

[8] Committee on Ethics, *In the Matter of Allegations Relating to Representative Luis V. Gutierrez,* H. Rept. 112-192, 112th Cong. 1st Sess. (2011).

[9] Committee on Ethics, *In the Matter of Todd Poole,* H. Rept. 112-203, 112th Cong. 1st Sess. (2011).

[10] Committee on Ethics, *In the Matter of Allegations Relating to Representative Don Young,* H. Rept. 112-336, 112th Cong. 1st Sess. (2011).

[11] Committee on Ethics, *In the Matter of Allegations Relating to Representative Laura Richardson,* H. Rept. 112-642, 112th Cong. 2d Sess. (2012).

[12] Committee on Ethics, *In the Matter of Allegations Relating to Representative Vernon G. Buchanan,* H. Rept. 112-588, 112th Cong. 2d Sess. (2012).

[13] Committee on Ethics, *In the Matter of Allegations Relating to Representative Shelley Berkley,* H. Rept. 112-716, 112th Cong. 2d Sess. (2012).

[14] Committee on Ethics, *In the Matter of Regarding Arrests of Members of the House During a Protest Outside the Embassy of Sudan in Washington, DC, on March 16, 2012,* H. Rept. 112-419, 112th Cong. 2d Sess. (2012).

[15] *See, e.g.,* House Committee on Standards of Official Conduct, *In the Matter of Representative Earl F. Hilliard,* H. Rept. 107-130, 107th Cong. 1st Sess. (2001); House Committee on Standards of Official Conduct, *In the Matter of Representative Jay Kim,* H. Rept. 105-797, 105th Cong. 2d Sess. at 6, 677 (1998).

[16] Committee on Ethics, *In the Matter of Joy Henrichs,* H. Rept. 112-696, 112th Cong. 2d Sess. (2012).

[17] Committee on Ethics, *In the Matter of Representative Tim Ryan,* H. Rept. 112-710, 112th Cong. 2d Sess. (2012).

INDEX

A

B

C

D

E